Living in France

Teach® Yourself

Living in France

Peter MacBride

with

Monique Perceau

For UK order enquiries: please contact Bookpoint Ltd, 130 Milton Park, Abingdon, Oxon OX14 4SB. Telephone: +44 (0)1235 827720. Fax: +44 (0)1235 400454. Lines are open 09.00–17.00, Monday to Saturday, with a 24-hour message answering service. Details about our titles and how to order are available at www.teachyourself.co.uk.

Long renowned as the authoritative source for self-guided learning – with more than 50 million copies sold worldwide – the **teach yourself** series includes over 500 titles in the fields of languages, crafts, hobbies, business, computing and education.

British Library Cataloguing in Publication Data.
A catalogue record for this title is available from The British Library.

Library of Congress Catalog Number: on file.

First published in UK 2005 by Hodder Education, 338 Euston Road, London, NW1 3BH. Previously published as *Buying a home in France* and *French for Homebuyers*.

This edition published 2010.

The **teach yourself** name is a registered trade mark of Hodder Headline Ltd.

Typeset by MacDesign, Southampton

Printed in Great Britain for Hodder Education, an Hachette Livre UK Company, 338 Euston Road, London NW1 3BH by Cox & Wyman Ltd, Reading, Berkshire.

Hodder Headline's policy is to use papers that are natural, renewable and recyclable products and made from wood grown in sustainable forests. The logging and manufacturing processes are expected to conform to the environmental regulations of the country of origin.

Impression number   10 9 8 7 6 5 4 3 2 1

Year   2014 2013 2012 2011 2010

contents

v

preface

The thought behind this book is a simple one. If you want to buy a house in France, it helps if you know the words. This isn't the same as being able to speak French – even with a degree in French, you probably won't know your *acte de vente* (contract of sale) from your *avant toit* (eaves). No, you don't actually have to be able to speak French – though it helps no end if you do – but if you know the words that describe houses and their various components, and the words that are involved in the sale process, then you will be better equipped for finding, buying and settling into your French home.

Living in France covers around 750 of the most useful words for home buyers and home owners, but this book is not a dictionary. A translation alone is sometimes not enough. It doesn't get you much further to know that *notaire* translates to 'notary', or that *espagnolette* means 'shutter fastener'. You need to know what the *notaire*'s role is and how it affects you, and what an *espagnolette* looks like. The words are given here in the context of the buying process or of different aspects of the house. Where it will help, I've tried to explain the concepts behind the words or to give an illustration.

I couldn't have produced this book without the assistance of my collaborator, Monique Perceau, and illustrator Tony Jones of Art Construction. Many thanks are also due to Ginny Catmur at Hodder, and Catherine MacGregor, my copy-editor; and in France to Robert Quarman, *bricoleur extraordinaire*, Linda, Béatrice and Chantal, *immobilières*, Benoit and the guys at *Bricomarché*, and to my friends and neighbours in Miramont.

Peter MacBride
Southampton and Miramont de Guyenne, 2007

x	**The CD**

The CD that accompanies this book is designed to be used alongside Chapter 10, *Une heure de français – an hour of French*. There are 20 tracks:

Track 1 is a very brief introduction to the French language, covering pronunciation, how to greet people, ask questions and understand simple replies.

The remaining tracks all give practice in speaking and listening to some of the most important or useful words in each chapter. It should take between 5 and 15 minutes to complete each one – work through a track before going out to tackle a job and you will be better prepared to deal with the *agents* and the *ouvriers*.

Track 2 links to Chapter 1, *La recherche – the search*

Track 3 links to Chapter 2, *La vente – the sale*

Track 4 links to Chapter 3, *Les travaux – building work*

Tracks 5–7 link to Chapter 4, *La structure – the structure*

Track 5: *Talking to le maçon – the builder*

Track 6: *Finding tools and materials at the bricolage*

Track 7: *Talking to le charpentier – the roof carpenter – and le couvreur – the roofer*

Tracks 8–10 link to Chapter 5, *La menuiserie – woodwork*

Track 8: *Talking to le menuisier – the joiner*

Track 9: *Finding materials at the bricolage*

Track 10: *Finding tools at the bricolage*

Tracks 11–13 link to Chapter 6, *La plomberie – plumbing*

Track 11: *Talking to le plombier – the plumber*

Track 12: *Shopping for bathroom and kitchen equipment*

Track 13: *Finding tools at the bricolage*

The voices on the CD are those of Katherine Pageon and Stuart Nurse.

01

la recherche
– the search

Almost the same...

There was a time when most houses were sold directly by the owner, working with a *notaire* (lawyer). You will still sometimes see hand-written *à vendre* signs tacked to shutters or to a post in the garden, and notaires still advertise and sell houses for their clients, but most houses now are sold through *agents immobiliers* (estate agents). This can make the search simpler for us overseas buyers.

French agents are almost the same as those in the UK. The most visible difference is that they are tight-fisted with their information sheets – you can't call them handouts if they aren't handed out! In the UK, you can walk into any agency, help yourself to sheets on as many houses as you like, and take them away to study at your leisure. In a typical French agency you will see a selection of sheets in the window, and perhaps inside. When you enter, you will be offered a loose-leaf file to browse through at a desk. The sheets tend to have less information than those of UK agents, but what the *immobiliers* don't put on the sheets, they keep in their notes and in their heads. The staff seem to know their properties and can talk intelligently about them. If you find any that interest you, they will arrange a visit. (And if you insist, they might make you a photocopy of the sheet!)

But before we get into an agent's office, we have to find one! Let's start the search.

Define your search

Where do you want to buy a house? In which region? In a town, a village or in the countryside? What sort and size of house do you want? How much garden? How much work do you want to have to do on it? Are you looking for a ruin to rebuild, an old house to restore, one that needs a little light redecorating, or a new build? These are questions that only you can answer – the checklist on page 4 may help you to define your ideal house.

If you don't know where you want to be, or what sort of house, spend more time exploring France, renting different types of houses in different areas, then start looking.

BOURSE DE L'IMMOBILIER

Placez-vous sous notre aile

A VENDRE

REGION PELLEGRUE

**Maison de village
comprenant cuisine équipée, salon/séjour avec
cheminée ancienne, 2 chambres, dressing,
salle d'eau, wc, véranda, buanderie
Dépendance attenante d'environ 60 m2
Dépendance non attenante d'environ 50 m2
Joli jardin avec vue sur la campagne. Puits**

124 000,00 €   **813 387 F**

N° du Mandat : 214D01
Réf. catalogue : 119-279

Frais d'agence inclus
-> 119

An information sheet from an agent immobilier. These typically have a good colour photo of the house, showing its best aspect, a list of the rooms and brief details of the garden, pool, garage and any outbuildings. Notice that prices are shown in euros and francs – but that the French use different punctuation in numbers. They use commas for decimal points, and spaces for commas. This house was for sale at €124,000 (about £85,000). And notice the small print – Frais d'agence inclus means that the agency's fees are included in the price.

Ideal house checklist

Location: Region or département..

Town, village or countryside?.............................

Is the view important?...

Max. distance from shops ....

Max. distance from cafés/restaurants ....

Max. distance from airport/sea port ....

Max. distance from beach/swimming, etc.

Max. distance from children's play facilities ....

Size: Number of bedrooms ....

Other rooms..

Min. total floorspace (1) ....

Outside: Swimming pool? (Y/N)...

Garage/parking needed? (Y/N) ....

Min. garden/land area...

Condition: New build, or an existing house? (2) ....

Ruin/renovation/redecoration/ready? (3) ....

What furniture/fittings are present? ....

Budget: How much money is available?............................

How much time do you have? (4) ....

(1) The size of a house is normally expressed in total floor area. A cottage or small terraced house is around 50m², 100m² is equivalent to a typical new British semi, 200m² is the size of an older 5-bed detached house in the UK.

(2) Notaire's fees and taxes will add approx. 5% to the cost of a new house or 10% to the cost of an older one (page 41).

(3) If you plan to rebuild or restore, you must have some idea of the cost of building work and be prepared to deal with the paperwork (see Chapter 3).

(4) The less time you have to work on the house, the more professional services you will have to buy.

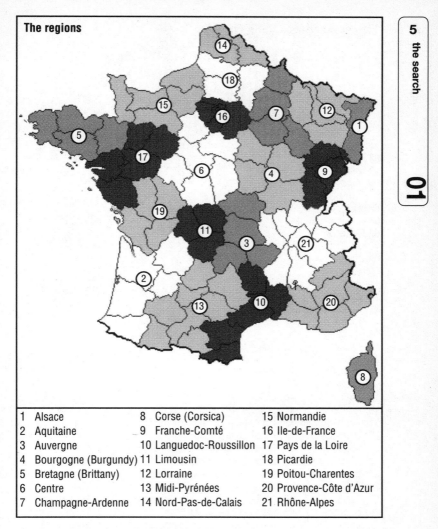

The regions

1	Alsace	8	Corse (Corsica)	15	Normandie
2	Aquitaine	9	Franche-Comté	16	Ile-de-France
3	Auvergne	10	Languedoc-Roussillon	17	Pays de la Loire
4	Bourgogne (Burgundy)	11	Limousin	18	Picardie
5	Bretagne (Brittany)	12	Lorraine	19	Poitou-Charentes
6	Centre	13	Midi-Pyrénées	20	Provence-Côte d'Azur
7	Champagne-Ardenne	14	Nord-Pas-de-Calais	21	Rhône-Alpes

The regions and departments of France

The numbers on the regional map (above) are simply there to label the map neatly. The numbers on the department map (next page) are quite different. The numbers (and the name) of departments were organized by Napoleon, the great codifier, and are an integral part of how the French think of their country.

Les départements

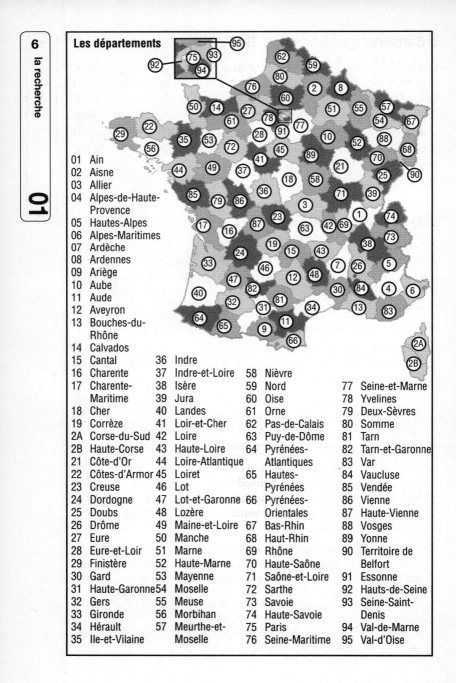

01 Ain
02 Aisne
03 Allier
04 Alpes-de-Haute-
   Provence
05 Hautes-Alpes
06 Alpes-Maritimes
07 Ardèche
08 Ardennes
09 Ariège
10 Aube
11 Aude
12 Aveyron
13 Bouches-du-
   Rhône
14 Calvados
15 Cantal

16	Charente	36	Indre		
17	Charente- Maritime	37	Indre-et-Loire	58	Nièvre
18	Cher	38	Isère	59	Nord
19	Corrèze	39	Jura	60	Oise
2A	Corse-du-Sud	40	Landes	61	Orne
2B	Haute-Corse	41	Loir-et-Cher	62	Pas-de-Calais
21	Côte-d'Or	42	Loire	63	Puy-de-Dôme
22	Côtes-d'Armor	43	Haute-Loire	64	Pyrénées- Atlantiques
23	Creuse	44	Loire-Atlantique		
24	Dordogne	45	Loiret	65	Hautes- Pyrénées
25	Doubs	46	Lot		
26	Drôme	47	Lot-et-Garonne	66	Pyrénées- Orientales
27	Eure	48	Lozère		
28	Eure-et-Loir	49	Maine-et-Loire	67	Bas-Rhin
29	Finistère	50	Manche	68	Haut-Rhin
30	Gard	51	Marne	69	Rhône
31	Haute-Garonne	54	Moselle	70	Haute-Saône
32	Gers	55	Meuse	71	Saône-et-Loire
33	Gironde	56	Morbihan	72	Sarthe
34	Hérault	57	Meurthe-et- Moselle	73	Savoie
35	Ile-et-Vilaine			74	Haute-Savoie
				75	Paris
				76	Seine-Maritime

77	Seine-et-Marne
78	Yvelines
79	Deux-Sèvres
80	Somme
81	Tarn
82	Tarn-et-Garonne
83	Var
84	Vaucluse
85	Vendée
86	Vienne
87	Haute-Vienne
88	Vosges
89	Yonne
90	Territoire de Belfort
91	Essonne
92	Hauts-de-Seine
93	Seine-Saint- Denis
94	Val-de-Marne
95	Val-d'Oise

Searching through the Web

Get online before you leave home and give yourself a head start. You may be able to find your French house through the Web – I did – but even if you don't find a specific one, you will find the more active agents and get a good idea of the prices in an area.

If you miss out the Web search, you will spend the first days of your visit hunting through the *Pages Jaunes* (Yellow Pages) or the town itself looking for the agents immobiliers.

There are four main types of sites:

UK-based property sites

As well as advertising houses, these offer varying levels of help with buying and settling in, e.g. arranging mortgages, translating legal documents, linking with English-speaking craftsmen. The main limitation, of course, is that they only have a tiny proportion of the houses on the market.

Here are some UK-based sites that you may find useful:

FPS online advertises properties throughout France, but mainly in the south and west, and can help with arranging mortgages. Find them at: **www.frenchpropertyservice.com**

Assetz are specialists in investment in property overseas, and have a well-established French section. They are very clued up on mortgages, tax and legal matters. The address of the French section of their site is: **http://france.assetz.co.uk**

French Property News is the web site of the magazine for UK buyers. They host well-organised 'small ads' for a good number of UK or English-speaking agents, so a single search there can save you traipsing round the separate sites. Find them at **www.french-property-news.com**

Latitudes is based in the UK, but works with a network of French estate agents to give a comprehensive coverage of all of France. Their site is at **www.latitudes.co.uk**

Internet French Property also has a network of French agents offering a very wide selection of houses across the whole of France. Their advice pages are well worth reading. Visit them at **www.french-property.com**

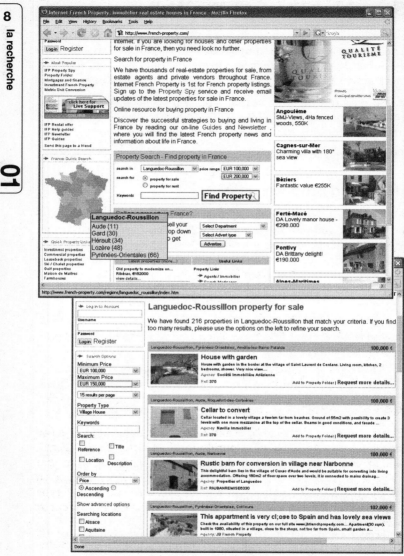

A quick search at Internet French Property. At the first stage you select the region and price range, or just click on the area. This produces a list of houses, with a tiny image, a brief description and a link to a fuller display (page 9). If you get too many – I found over 400 houses between €100,000 and €200,000 in Languedoc-Roussillon – you can refine the search.

Internet French Property usually provides a good set of photos showing the house from different views.

Les agents immobiliers – estate agents

Some *agents immobiliers* are national, some cover one or more departments and others are purely local. All the larger agents, and an increasing number of the small ones, have web sites, and most sites have a search facility. The searches vary, but tend to follow the same pattern – you will be asked to specify the type of property, price range and the region or department (except at a local agent's site).

At nationwide sites, a simple search can produce a lot of results. These sites usually have an advanced search page, where you can filter the selection by specifying a more limited price range, the number of rooms, amount of land and other options (different sites have different options).

These sites are all worth visiting:

Century 21 is the largest agency in France, boasting total sales of nearly €5,000,000,000 in 2003. They have over 700 offices, though they are not represented in every region. Make them your first stop at **www.century21france.fr**

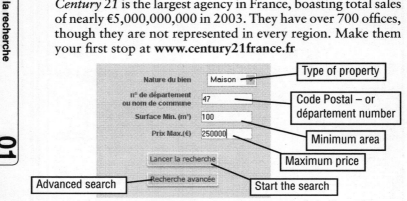

A simple search form – this is at Bourse de l'Immobilier.

Laforêt Immobilier is the second largest agency, with nearly 500 offices in France, and typically carrying around 25,000 properties. The site is available in English as well as French, and they offer a useful e-mail alert service, that will keep you posted of new properties matching your criteria. Find them at **www.laforet.com**

Bourse de l'immobilier has 125 offices nationwide, staffed by lovely people (they sold me my house). You can find them at **www.bourse-immobilier.fr**. Click on the *Acheter* (buying) link to reach the page to search for houses to buy.

FNAIM (Fédération Nationale des Agents Immobiliers) is a professional association with a membership of nearly 9,000 estate agents, large and small. It provides a range of services for its members, which need not concern us. What is interesting is its database, which has details of the properties handled by many of its members. The search form is on the top page at **www.fnaim.fr**

These last two are umbrella organisations, carrying small ads from both *immobiliers* and private sellers.

Le portail de l'immobilier at **www.nexdom.com**

Seloger at **www.seloger.com**

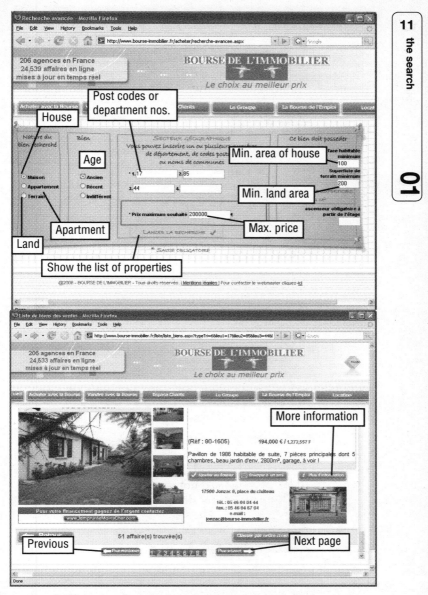

Searching at Bourse de l'Immobilier – the better sites all work in much the same way. With a little vocabulary you can run a search and make sense of the results. Click on Plus d'information for more details (see overleaf).

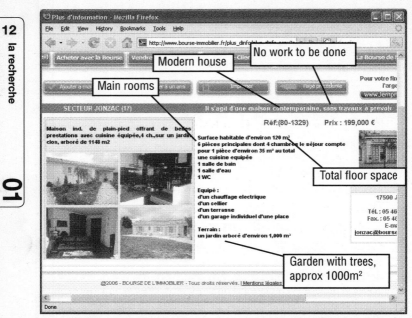

An example of the + d'infomation at the Bourse. Some agents tell you more, but this is enough to decide whether the house is worth a closer look.

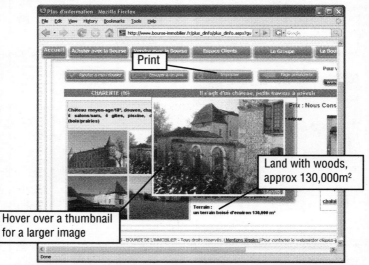

You'll find some great places on the Pages Prestiges! They don't give the price for this chateau, but if you have to ask, you probably can't afford it!

Local agents immobiliers

Not all *agents immobiliers* have web sites, but you can still use the Web to find the ones in your area. *Immosearch*, at **www.immosearch.tm.fr**, has lists of agents, organised by region. The lists are accessible, but not comprehensive. You can find much fuller lists at *Les Offres Immobilières*, at this address: **http://www.offres-immo.com/Annuaires/index.htm**.

Of course, you can google for the local agents. Go to *Google*, at **www.google.com**, and type in '*immobilier*' and the name of the town or department. You will have to do some filtering, but could find some good leads in the resulting links.

Agents as searchers

Some agents, such as Laforêt, offer e-mail update services, that will compare your search criteria against new properties and alert you of any that may be suitable. Others will invite you to send your requirements by e-mail, and will search beyond the properties visible on-line to try to find one to suit you – this service is often offered by UK-based sites and by English-speaking agents in areas popular with UK buyers. You may have to pay for this, either in actual fees or in higher property prices, but it may be worth it, especially if you are short of time for searching on the ground.

Notaires as agents

The *notaires'* professional organisation, *Notaires de France*, runs a web site at **www.notaires.fr**. The site has an English version – click the little Union Jack when you first arrive to switch to it. There are three good reasons for visiting:

- *Notaires* advertise houses here. The coverage is patchy, for example, I found a good selection of (expensive) houses in the Côte d'Azur, but hardly any, at any price, in Languedoc.

- There's lots of advice and information.

- You can find the *notaires* in an area. It may be worth contacting them, to see if they have any suitable houses. And you may want to have your own *notaire* to handle the sale. (Normally both parties use the same one, see page 30.)

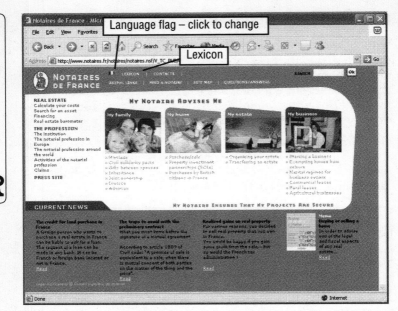

The English version of the Notaires de France site, seen here at the top page. There is a good lexicon of legal terms, very informative articles and booklets on different aspects of house buying.

Search on the ground

When you plan your buying trip, allow at least twice as much time as you think is really necessary. Delays can happen, and if everything does goes smoothly, you can relax and treat the rest of your stay as a simple holiday.

If you find potential houses on the Web, contact the agents or *notaires* by e-mail or phone to arrange to visit them. Allow plenty of time for each visit. The agencies may have other properties – newly-in or not advertised online – that you may want to see, and each house viewing can take a while.

Use the *Pages Jaunes* (Yellow Pages) directory to find the other local agents and notaires and see what they have to offer. Look out for the free property advertising brochures – many agencies have a rack by the door. And keep an eye out for *à vendre* (for sale) signs outside houses.

Two à vendre signs spotted by the roadside: a brief but very visible AV.

This was less visible, and less welcoming – 'curieux s'abstenir' can be best translated as 'no time-wasters'.

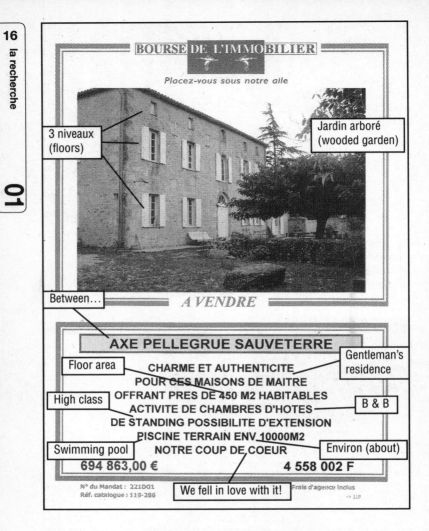

BOURSE DE L'IMMOBILIER

Placez-vous sous notre aile

3 niveaux (floors)

Jardin arboré (wooded garden)

Between…

A VENDRE

AXE PELLEGRUE SAUVETERRE

Floor area

Gentleman's residence

CHARME ET AUTHENTICITE
POUR CES MAISONS DE MAITRE
OFFRANT PRES DE 450 M2 HABITABLES
ACTIVITE DE CHAMBRES D'HOTES
DE STANDING POSSIBILITE D'EXTENSION
PISCINE TERRAIN ENV 10000M2
NOTRE COUP DE COEUR

High class

B & B

Swimming pool

Environ (about)

694 863,00 €   **4 558 002 F**

We fell in love with it!

N° du Mandat : 221D01
Réf. catalogue : 119-286

Frais d'agence inclus
-> 119

An immobilier's brochure for a house, though this maison de maître (gentleman's residence) has been turned into a business – activité de chambres d'hôtes means bed & breakfast. The agency was very taken with it. They are promoting this as their coup de coeur – they fell in love with it.

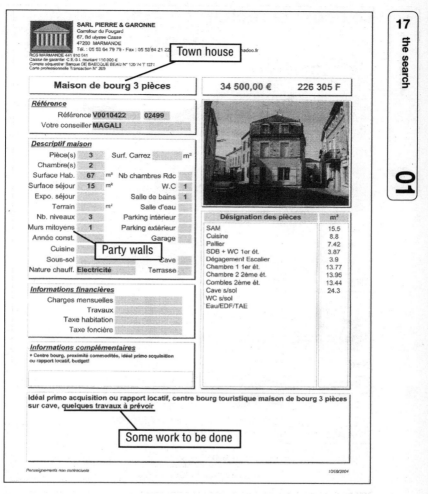

SARL PIERRE & GARONNE
Carrefour du Fougard
67, Bd ulysse Casse
47200 MARMANDE
Tél. : 05 53 64 79 79 - Fax : 05 53 64 21 22
RCS MARMANDE 441 810 041
Caisse de garantie C.E.G.I. montant 110 000 €
Compte séquestre Banque DE BARROQUE BEAU N° 120 74 T 1271
Carte professionnelle Transaction N° 269

Town house

Maison de bourg 3 pièces	34 500,00 €	226 305 F

Référence

Référence **V0010422** 02499
Votre conseiller **MAGALI**

Descriptif maison

Pièce(s)	3	Surf. Carrez	m²
Chambre(s)	2		
Surface Hab.	67 m²	Nb chambres Rdc	
Surface séjour	15 m²	W.C	1
Expo. séjour		Salle de bains	1
Terrain	m²	Salle d'eau	
Nb. niveaux	3	Parking intérieur	
Murs mitoyens	1	Parking extérieur	
Année const.		Garage	
Cuisine			
Sous-sol		Cave	
Nature chauff.	Electricité	Terrasse	

Party walls

Désignation des pièces	m²
SAM	15.5
Cuisine	8.8
Pallier	7.42
SDB + WC 1er ét.	3.87
Dégagement Escalier	3.9
Chambre 1 1er ét.	13.77
Chambre 2 2ème ét.	13.95
Combles 2ème ét.	13.44
Cave s/sol	24.3
WC s/sol	
Eau/EDF/TAE	

Informations financières

Charges mensuelles	
Travaux	
Taxe habitation	
Taxe foncière	

Informations complémentaires

+ Centre bourg, proximité commodités, idéal primo acquisition
ou rapport locatif, budget!

Idéal primo acquisition ou rapport locatif, centre bourg touristique maison de bourg 3 pièces
sur cave, quelques travaux à prévoir

Some work to be done

Renseignements non contractuels   10/09/2004

This house is at the other end of the scale. Potentially it could be a very smart
town house – it is in a prominent position at the end of the main street, and
even has brackets on the wall to take the flags on high days and holidays.
But when they said quelques travaux à prévoir (some work to be done), they
meant it.

This agency gives more detail on the brochure than most, but a picture large
enough to show the cracks and the crumbling tiles would have saved me an
hour's drive!

Lexicon: la recherche – the search

achat (m)*	purchase
acheter	to buy
affiner les critères	modify (search criteria)
agent (m) immobilier	estate agent
à vendre	for sale
lancer la recherche	start the search
maison (f)*	house
pièce (f)	room
précédent	previous
récent	modern
recherche (f)	search
suivant	next
terrain (m)	land (for building)
travaux à prévoir	work to be done

* All nouns are either masculine (m) or feminine (f) – see page 174

Immobilier abbreviations

bat	bâtiment	building
bur	bureau	office
cc	chauffage central	central heating
chs	chambres	bedrooms
pl/p/pp	plat/plein pied	single storey
p prin	pièces principales	main rooms
rdc	rez-de-chaussée	ground floor
sal	salle de séjour	lounge
sam	salle à manger	dining room
sdb	salle de bains	bathroom
sde	salle d'eau	bathroom
sej	séjour	lounge
sh	surface habitable	floor area
T1, T2...	Type 1, Type 2...	number of rooms, used to describe flats

New houses

The French themselves generally prefer new houses to 'second hand' ones – and there is a lot to be said in their favour. New houses have new fully-fitted kitchens and bathrooms; they will be freshly painted and decorated throughout to your specifications; and if you have been involved from an early enough stage, the layout and the number, size and types of rooms may have been customised to your liking. And, of course, if you start from scratch with a plot of land and your own builder, then the house will be exactly as you want it (if all goes to plan...).

All new houses have a ten-year warranty (*garantie décennale*), and there are some financial advantages of buying a new home. The deposit is 5%, instead of the normal 10%, the registration fees are lower, and the house is exempt from property tax for two years. Unfortunately, new houses are subject to VAT – which is currently 19.6% in France. When you are quoted a price for a new house, ask if it includes VAT (*TVA = Taxe sur la Valeur Ajoutée*).

The property sites and immobiliers deal with new houses as well as old ones, but there are also those who specialise in new builds. If you want the sort of French house that the French build for themselves, have a look at the Terrebonne site at **www.immobilier-terrebonne.com**

Buying for investment?

Some people do buy houses in France more as investments than for their own use, hoping for capital growth or rental income or both. If this is your plan, you should be aware of the following. House prices have been as volatile there, as they have been in the UK, though they do seem to be recovering from the 2008 collapse. The euro is unstable at the time of writing (summer 2010) so the actual cost in pounds could vary significantly between the time of agreeing the pruchase (in euros) and the time of paying for it. There is currently a lot of spare capacity in the holiday rental market – bookings have fallen and more people are offering property – though there are leaseback schemes that offer guaranteed rental income.

There's more on buying property for investment in the Appendix (page 197).

Lexicon: les genres des maisons – types of houses

aménageable	could be converted
ancien	old
belle vue	beautiful view
bien	property
bon état	good condition
bord de mer/rivière	by the sea/river
campagne	country
chalet (m)	chalet – wood or wood on stone house in Alpine regions
château (m)	castle, country residence – not necessarily fitted with turrets and battlements, a 'château' may be a big farmhouse with a courtyard and pretentions
colombage	half-timbered (similar to Tudor-style, but normally genuinely old)

Château, Limousin – quite a small one (only 10 bedrooms), but with a 12th century tower and terrific views out the back. Ah, if only…

demeure (f)	residence
domicile (m)	house/home
ferme (f)	farmhouse
fermette (f)	small farmhouse, cottage
grange (f)	barn
longère (f)	'long house' – single storey farmhouse typical of Brittany
maison (f)	house
maison bourgeoise	'middle class' – substantial, good quality town house
maison de campagne	country house
maison de maître	gentleman's house
maison individuelle	detached house
manoir (m)	manor house
mitoyenne	semi-detached or terraced
moulin (m)	mill

The old and the new – two colombage town houses, with breezeblock infill, Périgord. They wouldn't get away with that infill now (see Chapter 3).

pavillon (m)	modern house
pigeonnier (m)	pigeon loft – often large enough to make a decent room
à rénover	for renovation
rénové	renovated
à restaurer	for restoration (this can mean complete rebuild!)
ruine (f)	ruin – expect to knock it down and start from scratch
tout à l'égout	mains drains

Partly restored ferme (farmhouse) with attached grenier (barn), Gironde. As is often the case, the barn is almost as large as the house. Inside it is effectively a single space which could be divided and laid out in many different ways – though the walls are so thick that every new window will be a major operation to install.

En viager

When a house is sold en viager, the ownership does not pass to the buyer until the death of the seller. It is an arrangement which provides a pension to the elderly who want to augment their income and have no heirs to worry about. There is usually a small initial lump sum, and the annual payment is typically fairly low – though index-linked – but there is no knowing how long the buyer will have to wait. Viagers have outlived their buyers before now!

Lexicon: les pièces et les aménagements – rooms and facilities

agrandissement (m)	extension
alimentation (f)	supply (water, electricity, etc.)
aménagement de grenier	loft conversion
bureau (m)	study/office
cabinet (m)	small room
cabinet de travail	study
cabinet WC	lavatory
cave (f)	cellar
cellier (m)	storeroom
chambre (f)	bedroom
charges comprises	service charges included
cheminée (f)	chimney, also refers to fireplace
cour (f)	courtyard
cuisine (f)	kitchen
cuisine américaine	open-plan kitchen
dépendance (f)	outbuilding
étage (m)	first floor

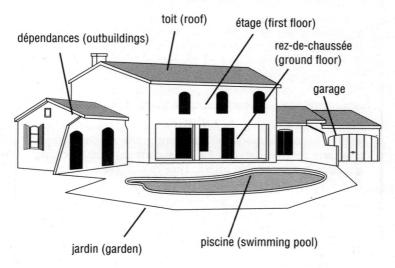

toit (roof)

étage (first floor)

dépendances (outbuildings)

rez-de-chaussée (ground floor)

garage

jardin (garden)

piscine (swimming pool)

fosse (f) septique	septic tank
garage (m)	garage
grenier (m)	attic/loft
jardin (m)	garden
logement	accommodation
piscine (f)	swimming pool
propriétaire (m)	owner
propriété (f)	property
rez-de-chaussée (m)	ground floor
salle (f)	room
salle de bains	bathroom
salle à manger	dining room
salle de séjour/le séjour	living room/lounge
salon (m)	dining room
sous-sol (m)	basement
terrain (m)	grounds
toit (m)	roof

What's included in the price?

If the house is furnished when you view it, ask very carefully about what will be included in the sale price. It is normal in France for the vendor to remove everything that isn't screwed down and quite a lot of what is. The bath, toilet and other sanitaryware are usually left, but the kitchen fittings – including the sink – may be taken, along with garden ornaments, shelves, carpets, curtains, light bulbs...

If there is anything in the house that you would like to be there when it becomes yours, tell the agent or the vendor, agree a price and get it written into the initial contract. Most vendors are open to reasonable offers. They're not trying to rip you off – it's just a different way of doing things.

Found it?

You've found a house that's perfect, or as near as perfect as you can get within your budget. What next? There are three key questions that need answering:

- Is the house worth the asking price?

- Is it really within your budget?

- If you intend to adapt, improve or extend the house, will you be allowed to do it?

To get the answers, ask the experts.

L'expert immobilier – the valuer

Experts immobiliers are called on to value houses not just for purchases, but also as required in divorce settlements and other legal disputes. Their valuation will be based on:

- The prices of other houses sold recently in the same area.

- The condition of the house and the cost of essential improvements, e.g. new roof, installation of a septic tank, connection to mains drains, water, gas or electricity, and the like.

- The land owned with the property. Old houses, especially in villages, often have one or more non-adjacent gardens or other plots of land. The expert will check the *cadastre* – the official map that shows the boundaries and ownership of land in the commune.

- The planning status of the area, as shown in the commune's *POS* (*Plan d'Occupation des Sols*) – planning brief. This will tell you what future development may happen in the area around the house, and whether you will be able to adapt it in the way you want to. We will have another look at the *POS* in Chapter 3.

- Any rights of way or other encumbrances on the property.

You can find an expert at their web site (**www.experts-fnaim. org**) or by post at:

Chambre des Experts Immobiliers de France
129 rue du Faubourg St-Honoré
75008 Paris

Les devis – estimates

If there are limited jobs to do on the house, e.g. a new roof, new bathroom, rewiring or similar, you can ask local tradesmen for a *devis* (estimate). You can rely on a *devis* to give you an accurate cost of the finished work – as long as you take it up within a few months, and don't redefine the job. If there is more complicated work to be done, approach a *maître d'oeuvre* (master of the works). This is someone who can organise a building job, and will get estimates and draw up plans for you. We will come back to the *maître d'oeuvre* and *devis* in Chapter 3 when we look at building work.

Do you need a valuation?

You do not have to have a valuation – it is optional. If you are buying a town house or apartment, in good condition and for a petit prix (low price) – and you can still find these places – a valuation is only essential if you are taking out a mortgage, or if you want reassurance about the price.

English–French quick reference

The search – la recherche

buy	acheter
estate agent	agent immobilier
for sale	à vendre
house	maison (f)
land (for building)	terrain (m)
modern	récent
modify (the search)	affiner or modifier les critères
next	suivant
previous	précédent
room	pièce (f)
search	recherche (f)
start (the search)	lancer (la recherche)
work to be done	travaux à prévoir

Types of houses – les genres des maisons

barn	grange (f)
beautiful view	belle vue
castle, country residence	château (m)
convert	aménager
country	campagne (f)
good condition	bon état
house	maison (f) or domicile (m) or demeure (f)
mains drains	tout à l'égout
manor house	manoir (m)
mill	moulin (m)
old	ancien
pigeon loft	pigeonnier (m)
renovate	rénover, restaurer
ruin	ruine (f)
semi-detached/terraced	mitoyenne

Rooms and facilities – les pièces et les aménagements

accommodation	logement (m)
attic	grenier (m)
basement	sous-sol (m)
bathroom	salle de bains
bedroom	chambre (f)
cellar	cave (f)
chimney	cheminée (f)
dining room	salle (f) à manger or salon (m)
extension	agrandissement (m)
fireplace	cheminée (f)
first floor	étage (m)
garage	garage (m)
garden	jardin (m)
ground floor	rez-de-chaussée (m)

grounds	terrain (m)
half-timbered	colombage
kitchen	cuisine (f)
kitchen, open-plan	cuisine américaine
lavatory	cabinet WC
living room	salle de séjour/le séjour
loft	grenier (m)
outbuilding	dépendance (f)
owner	propriétaire (m)
property	propriété (f), bien (m)
roof	toit (m)
room	salle (f) or pièce (f)
septic tank	fosse (f) septique
service charges included	charges comprises
storeroom	cellier (m)
study	bureau (m), cabinet de travail
supply (water, electricity)	alimentation (f)
swimming pool	piscine (f)

02

la vente – the sale

Almost the same...

When you buy a house in England or Wales, nothing is certain until you exchange contracts, close to the end of the process. In France you and the seller are both committed to the terms of the sale at the very beginning. You cannot be gazumped in France, neither buyer nor seller can renegotiate the price, nor can either of you back out without paying hefty compensation. A sale may be cancelled if agreed conditions are not met or if a mortgage cannot be obtained. It is also possible that the *commune* or SAFER will assert their pre-emptive rights to buy the property (see the box below). The whole process should take two to three months – about the same time as in the UK.

The role of a French lawyer, a *notaire*, is subtly different from that of a UK solicitor. A *notaire* is not there to represent your interests, but to ensure that the transfer of ownership is done fairly and properly – which is, of course, in your interests. It is quite normal for both parties to use the same *notaire* – there is no conflict involved, and there is less chance of communication problems and delays. If you want your own *notaire*, that is perfectly acceptable, and won't make any difference to the fees.

There are some differences on mortgages too. The authorities in France are more concerned than those in the UK that people should not over-extend themselves. French banks and finance houses will lend you a smaller proportion of the value of the property, and take your outgoings as well as your income into account when calculating the maximum loan.

Droits de préemption (pre-emptive rights)

Under French law, the local commune has a right to buy any house that is offered for sale, if its land is needed by the commune for redevelopment. If the house has more than 1 hectare of land, SAFER (Société d'Aménagément Foncier et d'Etablissement Rural), which has responsibilities for agriculture and rural life, also has pre-emptive rights. Before a property can be sold, the notaire must alert the commune, and/or SAFER to the sale and give them the opportunity to exercise their rights. This is normally just a formality, but it has to be done.

La propriété et la loi – ownership and the law

Who will own your house? And what do you want to happen when the owner or one of the owners dies? These are important questions because French property is subject to French inheritance law, even if you live in the UK.

Under French law you cannot disinherit your children – they are always entitled to at least a portion of it – but the spouse does not have an absolute right to any assets. If a person dies without a French *testament* (will), the spouse is only entitled to one quarter of the estate where there are children from a previous marriage, or if there are only children from the same marriage, the spouse can elect to receive one quarter of the estate or a life interest in the whole property. (If there are no children, the deceased's parents will inherit their share.)

Your children – or your parents – are your *héritiers réservataires* (reserved heirs) and are entitled to a *réserve légale* (legal reserve). This amounts to half of the estate if there is one child, two thirds if there are two and three quarters if there are three or more. If there are no children, each living parent receives one quarter. The rest of the estate can be freely disposed of. You can will to your spouse either:

- the residue of the estate;

- one quarter of the estate, with a life interest in the rest;

- a life interest in the whole estate.

These inheritance rules can create problems, especially where there are children from previous marriages. The question is, what can you do about it?

La propriété tontine – joint ownership

When the *acte de vente* (contract of sale) is being drawn up, you can ask for a clause to be inserted to specify joint ownership. Then if one of the purchasers dies, that share of the ownership passes directly to the survivor, and does not become part of the estate.

SCI (Société Civile Immobilière) – private property company

You can buy a house through a SCI, a company set up to own the property. The SCI's shareholders are usually members of the family or a group of friends who are buying a property together.

A SCI gives you more flexibility over inheritance or future ownership of the property. For example, parents can set up the SCI with themselves as majority shareholders, and in their wills leave sufficient shares to each other to ensure that the surviving spouse retains control of the SCI. If the heirs are unlikely to be able to share ownership of the property happily, it is easier to transfer shares in the SCI than to buy out part shares in a house. (Note that you cannot use a SCI to disinherit the reserved heirs – a will which tries to do this can be declared invalid in the French courts.)

Where friends want to pool their resources to buy a property, the SCI is a good solution. The company provides an ongoing vehicle for sharing expenses – and income if the property is rented out – and simplifies changes of ownership, should any party later want to drop out.

Buying through a SCI does incur some extra costs. The company must be set up, and it must present annual accounts. If the house is solely for the owners' use, the accounts should not be a major headache, but if it is rented then the SCI is liable for company tax and accounting becomes more complex and costly.

Take expert advice

In all matters legal and financial, this book aims to give general guidance only. If you have any doubts or queries about what is right for you, talk to a properly qualified French specialist before making any decisions.

La proposition d'achat – the agreement to buy

Having found a house that you like, agreed a price with the vendor, and decided on the form of ownership, it's time to start the buying process. At the first stage, the *immobilier* or *notaire* may ask you to sign a *proposition d'achat* (also called a *promesse d'achat*). These are more common in commercial purchases than in domestic ones, and are more likely to be used if you have not yet agreed the price with the vendor. Essentially it states that you are willing to buy the property at a given price. If the vendor accepts the offer, this proposition will be used as the basis of the contract of sale.

Le compromis de vente – the sale agreement

This is the most common form of initial contract. There are alternatives including *acte sous-seing privé* (private agreement) used where the *immobilier* is handling the transfer, and a *promesse de vente* (sale agreement) which is used more in commercial sales. All share the same principles and have similar characteristics.

The contract must contain the following information:

* *Désignation* (description) describing the property, its dimensions and related costs. If it is an apartment, it should clearly identify the *parties communes* (communal areas) and the *parties privatives* (areas private to the owner).

* The price and date of payments. If a property is bought off-plan (i.e. before or while it is being built), payments are made in stages as the building progresses.

* The amount of the deposit.

* A date for signing the deed of sale.

The contract may also contain *clauses suspensives* (conditions – see page 36), and should list any *servitudes* (rights of way or similar rights held by others over the land).

The initial contract is legally binding on both parties. It defines what is being sold, fixes the price and specifies any *clauses suspensives*, conditions that could affect the sale. Note carefully that the contract has a *clause pénale* (penalty clause). If you fail to complete the sale, without valid reason, the deposit will be paid to the vendor as compensation. And it could get worse – the disappointed vendor has the right to take you to court to make you complete the purchase.

At this stage, you pay a deposit, typically of 10%, and the property is taken off the market. The deposit must be in Euros, and if you do not yet have a French bank account, immediate payment may prove impossible. This should not be a problem. You can agree to pay within a set time, paying by bank transfer once you get back to the UK.

If you will be taking out a *hypothèque* (mortgage) to finance the purchase, the known details (how much you are borrowing and where you hope to borrow from) will be written into the contract. If you are buying outright, you will have to write into the contract – **yourself and in French** – words to the effect that you are not seeking a mortgage. If you later decide that you need a mortgage but cannot get one, you cannot use this failure to cancel the sale (see *Clauses suspensives* on page 36).

You will be asked to make an *élection de domicile* (statement of residence). This is for tax purposes – if this will be your primary residence, you will be subject to French income tax and social security contributions. If it is a secondary residence, you will only be liable for taxes on the property (see page 43).

While working through the contract, you should be shown, and asked to sign, these certificates from an *expert en état sanitaire de l'immobilier* (house health and safety expert):

- *diagnostic amiante santé* (asbestos safety report) to show that the house has been checked for the presence of asbestos;

- *diagnostic plomb* (lead) **or** *saturnisme* (lead-related illness) following a check for lead;

- *attestation parasitaire* (insect infestation report) to confirm that the house is free from termites – certain areas only.

At this stage you will also need to know the name of your *notaire*, if you intend to use a different one from the vendor.

Finally, you will have to sign, where it says *L'acquéreur* (the buyer), writing the phrase:

bon pour achat au prix et conditions ci-dessus

('good for purchase' – i.e. purchase agreed – at the price and conditions stated above).

When you get your copy of the document, you will find that the vendor will have signed *bon pour vente* (good for sale).

EXPERT EN ETAT SANITAIRE DE L'IMMOBILIER

Diagnostics termites, amiante, plomb, humidité, loi «Carrez», D.T.I.

SARL ALBA ET FILS

ETAT PARASITAIRE RELATIF A LA PRESENCE
DES TERMITES DANS UN IMMEUBLE
(Article 6 du décret n° 2000-613 du 3 juillet 2000)
(Arrêté du 10 août 2000)

MANDATAIRE : Mme CASANOVA Antoinette
PROPRIETAIRE : Mme CASANOVA Antoinette
NOTAIRE : Me GRUBERO FEAJRJUDER
PARTIES PRESENTES :
DATE D'EXPERTISE : 10 09 2004
NOM DU TECHNICIEN : Monsieur ALBA Alain

A - Désignation de l'immeuble

Localisation de l'immeuble

Département : LOT-ET-GARONNE
Commune : MIRAMONT DE GUYENNE 47800
Adresse : 312 avenue Soussial
Section cadastrale : A D
N° des parcelles : 28 A ← Identifies the plot on the cadastre (the property register of the commune)

Nature de l'immeuble

Immeuble bâti : ☒ OUI ☐ NON
Immeuble non bâti : ☒ OUI ☐ NON

B -Désignation du demandeur

Nom : CASANOVA
Prénom : Antoinette
Adresse : « le jacquiereur « 47800 ROUMAGNE

Qualité du demandeur

Propriétaire : ☒ OUI ☐ NON
Locataire : ☐ OUI ☒ NON
Autre : ☐ OUI ☒ NON

3, rue des Batailles – 47410 LAUZUN - ☎ 05.53.94.15.90 – Fax 05.53.94.39.43 – Port 06.08.23.57.02
SARL au capital de 8000 Euros – SIRET 448 300 236 00016 – Code NAF 452V – 448 300 236 RCS MARMANDE

The top page of one of the expert reports on my house. At least I don't have termites – they are a growing problem in France, particularly in the south, and the south west. Vendors of houses in affected areas must produce insect infestation reports.

Can your French cope?

You need good French to be able to cope with the legal and technical terminology in the contract and certificates. If you have any doubts about your ability to fully understand the documents, ask for copies, take them away and get them translated. Take advice from an English-speaking notaire or a UK solicitor who understands French law.

Don't sign anything lightly.

Clauses suspensives – suspensive conditions

If you are going to take out a mortgage, then the contract is automatically dependent upon achieving that, but you can also write into the contract other conditions which must be met for the contract to be valid. These might include the receipt of a satisfactory *certificat d'urbanisme* (zoning certificate) – the equivalent of outline planning permission – for your proposed building or rebuilding. Any conditions must be agreed by the vendor, and time limits will be imposed, if appropriate. Be realistic. It can take time to get full, detailed planning permission through (see Chapter 3).

Le délai de réflexion – the cooling-off period

After you and the vendor have signed the contract, and you have received a signed copy, you have seven days to change your mind. During this time the deposit sits in a special account with the *notaire* or the *immobilier*. If you decide to back out of the sale, your deposit will be returned and the matter ends there.

If you decide later that you do not want to complete, the penalty clause will be invoked.

Remember the penalty clause works both ways. If your vendor cancels the sale, you will get 10% of the price as compensation.

Lexicon: Le compromis – the initial contract

achat (m)	purchase
acheteur (m)	purchaser
acheteuse (f)	purchaser
acte (m) de vente	contract of sale
acte sous-seing privé	private agreement, alternative initial contract
amiante (m)	asbestos
attestation parasitaire	insect infestation report
bon pour achat	good for purchase, indicates buyer agrees to the terms
bon pour vente	good for sale, indicates vendor agrees to the terms
certificat d'urbanisme	town planning zoning certificate
clause (f) pénale	penalty clause
clauses suspensives	conditions to be met for the agreement to be valid
compromis (m) de vente	sale agreement
co-propriété (f)	co-ownership
délai (m) de réflexion	cooling-off period
désignation (f)	description of the property
droits (m) de préemption	pre-emptive rights (to buy)
élection (f) de domicile	statement of residence
frais (m) d'agence	agency fees – paid by seller
héritiers réservataires	reserved heirs, who must receive at least part of the estate
hypothèque (f)	mortgage
notaire (m)	notary, lawyer and public official
offre (f) d'achat	offer to buy, at a stated price – this is not a contract
offre de vente	offer to sell at a stated price – again, this not a contract
parties (f) communes	communal areas
parties privatives	private areas in apartment block

plomb (m)	lead
propriété tontine	joint ownership
promesse (f) d'achat	the agreement to buy
promesse de vente	sale agreement
proposition (f) d'achat	agreement to buy, reserves the property at an agreed price
réserve (f) légale	portion of estate which must pass to the reserved heirs
SAFER	Société d'Aménagément Foncier et d'Etablissement Rural – controls use of agricultural land
saturnisme (m)	lead-related illness
SCI	Société Civile Immobilière – private property company
vendeur (m)	seller
vendeuse (f)	seller
vente (f)	sale

Finance

Before the sale can be completed, the purchase money must be in the *notaire*'s account. There are three main ways to do this:

- You can transfer the cash from your UK bank account, converted into Euros, using interbank transfer. You will need to know the *notaire*'s bank and his account's IBAN (International Bank Account Number) to do this. The money will take between three and five days to reach its destination.

- Obtain from your UK bank a banker's draft in Euros and give this to the *notaire*.

- And the simplest solution. Open a bank account in France, transfer the necessary funds into it and give the *notaire* a French cheque. You will have to have a French bank account if you take out a French mortgage, and it will make your continuing life there much simpler. With a French account you can set up direct debits to pay the tax and utility bills and save a lot of trouble – being out of the country at the time is not an acceptable excuse for not paying a bill when it is due! It takes minutes to open a French bank account. All you need is your passport and proof of your (intended) address in France – you don't even need to put in any money. They will happily arrange to send your correspondence to your UK address if required.

Mortgages

French mortgages usually require foreign residents to provide at least 15% of the purchase price – up to 30% on leaseback properties. Interest rates are currently lower than in the UK, but there are additional costs to be taken into account. You must have life insurance, which will typically cost around 0.5% of the amount, the bank will charge 1% for arranging the mortgage, and the *notaire's* fees are higher if there is one.

French banks are more cautious in their lending than those in the UK. You cannot normally borrow more than four times your total income. More to the point, you cannot normally borrow so much that your total debt ratio – outgoings, including other loan repayments compared to net income – is higher than 33%. If your income is over £75,000 or you are asking for a mortgage of less than 60%, then the bank may allow a higher ratio.

Do you have the cash?

A mortgage can only cover the property itself, not the legal costs of buying it (up to 8%, see page 41), so you must have the cash for these too. For example, with a €100,000 house you would need at least €15,000 for the deposit and €8,000 for the fees and taxes. With all the other inevitable costs of moving and settling, you would be ill-advised to start out on the venture without at least €40,000 to hand.

If you take out a French mortgage, do bear in mind that not only do interest rates vary, exchange rates also vary. Four years ago the interest rate in France was around 3% and the exchange rate was fairly stable at around £1 = €1.45. At the time of writing the interest rate is around 4% and the exchange rate is £1 = €1.25, though six months ago it was down to £1 = €1.05. According to the papers, the Euro could be very unstable for some time yet.

A 25-year €100,000 mortgage now costs around £4,000 p.a. An increase of 1% in the interest rate, would increase it by a little over £400. A fall back down to 1.05 in the exchange rate would cost almost exactly the same.

If you have plenty of equity in your UK house, you could re-mortgage it to release funds for an outright purchase in France. If you do this, you must organise the remortgage before signing the initial contract, or have a clause suspensive written into it to cover the possibility of the remortgage not going through. The normal rule that the sale can be cancelled if a mortgage is not obtained does not apply here.

Whatever you do, take good advice and compare costs.

L'acte de vente – the contract of sale

Also referred to as *l'acte authentique* (genuine deed), this is the document that transfers ownership. In drawing it up, the *notaire* will have checked the vendor's right to sell, the boundaries of the property and any rights of way or restrictions on it. You will have been asked for a copy of your birth certificate, and if you are married, you will have had to confirm your marital status, as a spouse has rights in the house, however it is owned.

The *notaire*'s findings will be incorporated in *le projet d'acte* (the draft deed), which should be sent to you some time before the transfer day. This will give you a chance to have it translated and checked, if necessary, by a competent professional, and to raise any queries you may have.

The other thing you must do before the transfer day, is arrange to have *assurance* (insurance) in place. French law requires all houses to be insured, and if yours isn't the *notaire* will not allow the transfer to go ahead.

The *acte* is signed, with something of a ceremony, in the *notaire*'s office. Both the vendor and the purchaser are supposed to be there, though others can be given the power of attorney to sign for them.

The *notaire* will read through the document. The vendor and the purchaser both initial each page and sign the last page, with the phrase *bon pour accord* (agreed), to show that you have understood the document and that you agree its terms. Unless your French is very good, you are not likely to be able to follow the reading very well, but you should have understood the document from working through it at the draft stage. If required, the *notaire* can arrange for a translator to be present.

After signing, the *notaire* will give you a receipt for the purchase money, an *attestation de propriété* (certificate of ownership) or *attestation d'acquisition* (certificate of purchase), and the keys.

Le pouvoir – power of attorney

If it is not convenient for you to go – perhaps at very short notice – to the notaire's office to sign the contract, you can give someone a power of attorney to sign for you. This is quite commonly done by the French themselves. The power of attorney is typically assigned to one of the notaire's clerks, though never to the notaire. The document to set up the power of attorney must comply with French requirements, but is then signed before a notary public in the UK, to be authenticated.

That is the end of the ceremony, but the transfer is not quite complete yet. The *notaire* will send the signed deed to the local land registry for registration. This will take around two months. The document will be returned to the *notaire*, who will keep it, but give you an *expédition* (certified copy).

Fees and charges

Notaires perform a public function, and their fees are set by the state. They are non-negotiable, and there's no point in trying to shop around for a cheaper alternative. As transfer tax, registration costs and other official charges are also paid via the *notaire*, the total bill can be significant.

The fees and charges depend largely upon three things: the age of the property, its price and whether or not there is a mortgage.

◆ Houses less than five years old are not subject to transfer tax – but newly-built houses are subject to VAT.

- Houses over five years old are subject to transfer tax, which is currently 4.8%.

- The notaire's main fee is calculated from the price of the house – roughly 2% on the first €17,000 and 1% on the rest of the price. Further fees, called *émoluments* and *frais divers* (various fees), are due for various searches and formalities. These will total around €700.

- If there is a mortgage, a duty of 0.6% is due and the *notaire* receives a fee. This is on a sliding scale, from 0.6% to 1.5% – with the percentage falling as the mortgage increases.

- The *Conservateur Hypothèque* (register of mortgages) charges just over 0.1% of the house price if there is a mortgage, and exactly 0.1% if there isn't.

  The point of registering, whether there is a mortgage or not, is that it establishes the clear ownership of the property. When the *notaire* is drawing up the deeds, one of his jobs is to find out if a mortgage is held on the house and to make sure that it is cleared before the house is sold.

If you want to work out the legal fees, use an online calculator. There's one at **www.lesiteimmobilier.com** – and the site has an English version.

- If the notary handled the sale, he is due fees of 5% up to €46,000 and 2.5% over that. These fees may be paid by the seller or purchaser, depending upon the agreement.

- VAT is due on all the *notaire*'s fees.

For example, a property of €100,000 with a €75,000 mortage would result in these fees and charges:

Emoluments de notaire (notary fees)	€1,116
Emoluments sur prêt (loan fees)	€1,684
TVA (VAT)	€548
Droits de mutation (transfer tax)	€4,890
Droits sur prêt (duty on loan)	€461
Emoluments de formalités (fees for formalities)	€304
Frais divers (other fees)	€762
Conservateur Hypothèque (register of mortgages)	€137
TOTAL DES FRAIS (total fees)	**€9,902**

Without a mortgage, the fees for this house would be just over €7,000. If the house had been new, the transfer tax would have been only €500, saving €4,390.

If additional work is required, over and above the normal, then fees will be higher. For example, if the boundaries are unclear, then it may be necessary to employ a *géomètre* (surveyor) to clarify them.

Property taxes

There are four property taxes, not all of which may apply.

Taxe foncière (property tax)

This is a local tax that is paid by the owner of the house. The tax is not onerous; for example, on a *fermette* (farmhouse) in the Dordogne, you would expect to pay around €350 (£250) p.a. It is normal practice for the buyer to reimburse the seller for the tax for the remaining portion of the year.

Do note that this tax is based on the property's rentable value. If you buy a ruin and restore it to its former glory and beyond, the *taxe foncière* will go up appropriately.

Taxe d'habitation (occupation tax)

This is another local tax, but paid by the occupier. Unless you intend to rent out the house on a long-term basis, this will also be you. The charge is typically around 25% of the *taxe foncière*.

These taxes are both collected by the local *trésor public* (public revenue department), which will be in or close by the *mairie* (town hall). You can pay by post or over the counter when they fall due – normally October for the *taxe foncière* and November for the *taxe d'habitation* – or by *prélèvement automatique* (direct debit) through the year, starting from January.

There is a late payment penalty of 10%, and the *trésor public* will pursue you relentlessly!

Impôt sur la fortune (wealth tax)

This annual tax is only due if total value of your house and its contents is more than €720,000 at a rate of around 1%. I have no personal experience of this.

Taxe plus-value (capital gains tax)

This tax may be due when you sell the property. The total charge is normally 26% of the difference between what you paid for it – and what you spent on rebuilding, extending or other-wise improving it – and the price that you sell it for. If you sell in the first five years, the full amount is due. After five years, the amount of tax due is reduced by 1.6% each year, to 0% after 15 years.

Lexicon: la vente – the sale

acte (m) authentique	deed drawn up by a notaire
acte de vente	deed transferring property
assurance (f)	insurance
attestation d'acquisition	certificate of purchase
banque de consignation	the bank used by a notaire for the deposit of money
cadastre (m)	local register of land holdings
enregistrement (m)	registration of ownership
frais (m) de notaire	notary's fees

géomètre (m)	surveyor, who may be employed to confirm the boundaries of the property if they are not obvious
plan de cadastre	map showing land ownership
plus-value	capital gains on the sale of the property
prélèvement automatique	direct debit order
projet de l'acte	draft contract
taxe (f) d'habitation	local tax on occupation of property
taxe foncière	local tax on the property itself

Ask at the mairie

The mairie (local council) should be your first port of call for any questions about services, taxes or similar issues. If they don't deal with it themselves, they will usually be able to tell you who does. The mairie building may be labelled Hôtel de Ville (town hall).

Les services – services

Apart from water, utilities in France are all supplied by state-owned companies. The services are good, and the costs are comparable to or cheaper than in the UK – apart from water.

The utilities that are already connected to your house should be transferred to your name by the *agent immobilier* or *notaire* who is handling the sale. If they don't provide this service for you, contact the vendor and get the details of their contracts. It should be simple enough to get the *compte* (account) transferred to your name at the appropriate time. Getting connected to mains water, electricity, gas or telephone for the first time may be a bit more involved and take a little longer to achieve.

L'électricité – electricity

Electricity is supplied by EDF (Electricité de France). They have a wide range of tariffs – as we have in the UK, except this is all from one firm! The first thing to decide is how much power you need to have on tap. You need to choose the level of supply, from 3kVA to 36kVA, to match your possible peak demands. You can run the normal range of lights, TV, washing machine and other electrical applicances on a 9kVA supply, increasing to 12 or 15kVA if you are also using electricity as your main form of heating. The power level sets the *abonnement* (standing charge), but you pay the same price per kilowatt, except for the very lowest level of supply.

The electrical supply is 230 volts, as it is in the UK, but you will need buy adaptors – or change the plugs – to be able to use UK appliances in round-pin sockets. Buy French, it's easier!

EDF has a great system for working out what sort of tariff you need – almost entirely done in graphics, with minimal text.

Find out more about EDF at **www.edf.fr**. There is an English language version of the site – look for the link on the first page.

Le gaz – gas

Gas is supplied by GDF (Gaz de France), and they offer a bewildering range of tariffs, and the rates vary depending upon where you live. To give you a rough idea, where gas is used just to cook and heat the water, you might opt for a low user tariff,

Gaz and gaz de ville

Gaz de ville ('town gas', i.e. mains) is normally only available in towns – hence the name. If your house is in a rural area and you want gas for cooking and/or heating, you will have to use bottled gas. Supply is not a problem. Garages and supermarkets in rural areas normally sell gas.

paying €35 p.a. standing charge and 5 cents per kilowatt hour. If gas is also used for central heating – and it's a largish house in use for all or most of the year – then a high user tariff would be appropriate, and you would pay €180 p.a. but only 3 cents per kilowatt hour.

GDF is accessible online at **www.gazdefrance.fr**, but only in French and not as helpful.

For both gas and electricity, you really need to talk to EDF and GDF. You can do them both in one trip, as the firms are linked and share offices, though GDF is not always there. The best way to find your local office is to look in *Pages Jaunes* (Yellow Pages) or ask at the *mairie*. When I last tried, the EDF web site would tell you their local office – but only in the French version – and GDF didn't want online customers to know!

Le téléphone – telephone

If you decide that you need a landline telephone you should talk to France Télécom – find them at **www.agence.francetelecom.com**. It currently costs €49 to have a line installed, and the basic connection charge is €16 a month. There are many tariffs, including one for second homes, where you can suspend the service – and the charge – when you are not there.

A number of suppliers, including France Télécom, offer broadband (which the French call ADSL) and cable TV. Internet access alone will cost around €15 a month, on top of the phone line subscription. Internet + TV + telephone packages currently cost around €30 a month.

Les autres services – other services

Your *eau* (water) will be supplied by one of several companies – though there is no choice here, as only one is available in any area. The supply is metered, and the costs vary significantly. No supplier is cheap, and you should expect to pay up to €3 per cubic metre.

If your house is *tout à l'égout* (on mains drains), there will be an additional charge for waste water.

In towns, *les ordures* (rubbish) are collected from your *poubelle* (rubbish bin) in front of your house, several times a week – daily in big cities. In the countryside you must take your rubbish to the municipal bins, which may be some distance away.

Recyclage (recycling) provision varies, as it does in the UK. As here, you will find *conteneur à collecte de verre usagé* (bottle banks) and collection bins for paper, and perhaps more, in munipical and supermarket car parks and by the roadside.

Old furniture and appliances, building detritus and garden waste, hazardous materials and the like can all be disposed of in your local *déchetterie* (waste collection site) or *décharge* (dump).

Ask at the *mairie* to learn your collection days or to locate your nearest waste disposal sites.

Lexicon: les services – services

eau (f)	water
décharge (f)	rubbish dump
déchetterie (f)	waste collection site
hôtel (m) de ville	town hall (building)
mairie (f)	town hall (organisation)
ordures (f)	rubbish
Pages Jaunes	Yellow Pages
poubelle (f)	rubbish bin
recyclage (m)	recycling
tout à l'égout	on mains drains

English–French quick reference

The initial contract – le compromis

agency fees	frais (m) d'agence
agreed…	bon pour…
agreement to buy	promesse/proposition d'achat
asbestos	amiante (m)
conditional clauses	clauses suspensives
contract of sale	acte (m) de vente
cooling-off period	délai (m) de réflexion
co-ownership	co-propriété (f)
initial contract	compromis/promesse de vente, acte sous-seing privé
insect infestation report	attestation parasitaire
joint ownership	propriété tontine
lead	plomb (m)
mortgage	hypothèque (f)
notary	notaire (m)
offer to…	offre de…
penalty clause	clause pénale
pre-emptive rights	droits de préemption
private company	SCI, Société Civile Immobilière
purchase	achat (m)
purchaser	acheteur (m)/acheteuse (f)
reserved heirs	héritiers réservataires
seller	vendeur (m)/vendeuse (f)
statement of residence	élection de domicile
zoning certificate	certificat (m) d'urbanisme

The sale – la vente

capital gains	plus-values
certificate of purchase	attestation d'acquisition
deed of transfer	acte de vente, acte authentique

insurance	assurance (f)
land ownership map	plan de cadastre
land register	cadastre (m)
notary's fees	frais de notaire
registration of ownership	enregistrement (m)
surveyor	géomètre (m)
tax on occupation	taxe d'habitation
tax on property	taxe foncière

Services – les services

02

broadband	ADSL
electricity	électricité
gas	gaz
on mains drains	tout à l'égout
recycling	recyclage (m)
rubbish	ordures (f)
rubbish bin	poubelle (f)
rubbish dump	décharge (f)
telephone	téléphone
town hall	mairie (f), hôtel (m) de ville
waste collection site	déchetterie (f)
water	eau (f)

03

les travaux –
building work

Almost the same...

The French have planning permission and building regulations the same as we do in the UK, only more so. They control what can be built, where, its size, style and sometimes even its colour. I have to say that, by and large, it's a good idea. The controls help to preserve regional identities, to create more harmonious townscapes and to avoid blots on the countryside.

There are different levels of control:

◆ If you are going to build a new house, extend an existing one outwards or upwards, add a garage or a substantial outbuilding, you will need a *permis de construire* (building permit).

If the house to be built or modified has a total floor space of over 170 m², you must employ an architect.

◆ You only need to submit a *déclaration de travaux* (notice of works) if your planned alterations are significant but do not change the size of the building, or the house is *classé* (listed) or one close to a historic monument, or you intend to create an open swimming pool, or build a high wall.

◆ For small outbuildings (less than 2 m² and less than 1.5 m high), or walls less than 2 m high, no permissions are needed.

As in the UK, all building work is subject to local and national planning regulations, and to health and safety rules.

As well as buildings, the French also regulate builders more than we do. All registered tradesmen – and most are registered – must be properly qualified and their work carries a 10-year guarantee. This is definitely a good thing!

Check at the mairie

The *mairie* is central to all this. It's where the planning permits are issued, and it's where you will find list of registered tradesmen. In smaller communities, the *maire* (mayor) in person plays a significant role in this. It can take a longer or shorter time to get permissions agreed, and there can be more or fewer nits picked in the process. If you work with the *mairie* and the officials, and show that you want to be part of their community, it should make things go more smoothly.

Depending upon the size of your *commune*, there may be an architect or qualified officer in the *mairie* who can advise you on the regulations and how they apply to your project. If you cannot get help here, turn to the DDE. Each department has a *DDE (Direction Départementale de l'Equipement)* office which has overall planning control. On its staff you will find an *architecte conseil* (consultant architect) who will have responsibility for your *commune*. He can be consulted, free of charge.

POS – the planning brief

Almost all *communes* have a *code d'urbanisme* (town planning brief) and a *POS (Plan d'Occupation du Sol)* – a map that shows what use can be made of the land. These are the main land use categories:

◆ *UA (Urbaine A)*: town centre, with houses, shops and other services – usually has strict controls over size of buildings.

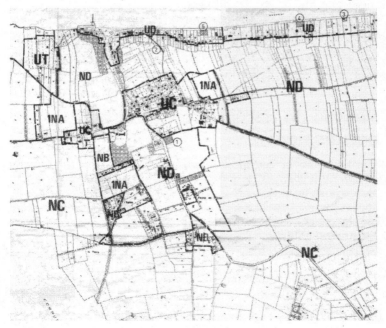

The POS of a small seaside commune. Here the main built-up area is all UC, with new building being allowed in the areas marked 1NA.

- *UB* and *UC*: mixed urban, high and low-density housing with some commercial and recreational activities.

- *UD*: urban, mainly low-density housing, typically on the outskirts of the town.

- *UE*, *UF*, *UG*, etc: commercial, industrial, recreational and other urban activities.

- *NA* (*Naturelle* A): currently rural, but may be urbanised over time. Ask for clarification if the house is in an NA zone.

- *NB* and *NC*: mainly agricultural use, strict controls over all building.

- *ND*: not usable, protected areas or those with high risk of natural disasters (flooding, etc.).

If you are buying a building plot, or a ruin that you intend to rebuild, check the *POS* map to make sure that the land falls into a suitable category. If you are buying in town, it's as well to check that any future developments won't alter the character of the neighbourhood – *UA* has most protection, but *UB*, *UC* and *UD* will remain residential.

Ask at the *mairie* to see the *POS*. The town's surveyor should be happy to show it to you.

Permis de construire – planning permission

The first step in getting a *permis* is to pick up a *formulaire demande de permis de construire* (form to request planning permission) from the *mairie*. There are several varieties of these. For building a new house or extending an existing one, you can use the general form or a *demande de permis de construire une maison individuelle*.

The form itself is quite complex, and must be accompanied by:

- a map showing the land's boundaries and its access roads, in the context of the *commune*;

- detailed plans of the house and drawings of it from each aspect and cross-sections, usually at 1:50 scale;

- a description of the materials to be used;

DEMANDE DE PERMIS DE CONSTRUIRE

CADRE RÉSERVÉ À L'ADMINISTRATION

DATE DE DÉPÔT
JOUR MOIS ANNÉE   58   PC   DÉPT COMMUNE ANNÉE N° DE DOSSIER

DEMANDEUR (le demandeur est le bénéficiaire de la future autorisation)

NOM, PRÉNOM OU DÉNOMINATION   NOM D'USAGE (le cas échéant)   TÉLÉPHONE

Qualité d' M/F

État, public d'M/F	Société, d'M/F autre immobilier constituée de protection	Société d'économie mixte	SCI ayant vocation vendre à la remmandre	Entreprise ou établissement à caractère industriel ou commercial	Collectivité locale	Particulier ou démembrement	Autre, personne morale	Particulier
1	2	3	4	5	6	7	8	9

ADRESSE (numéro, voie) :   Complément d'adresse

Code postal   Localité de destination

PERSONNE MORALE (Nom du représentant légal ou statutaire) :   PROMOTEUR IMMOBILIER (le cas échéant) NOM ou DÉNOMINATION

ADRESSE   TÉLÉPHONE

MAÎTRE D'OUVRAGE : La construction est-elle réalisée pour le compte de l'État, de la région ou du département, d'un établissement public ou concessionnaire de service public de l'une de ces collectivités, d'un État étranger ou d'une organisation internationale ? OUI ☐ NON ☐

TERRAIN (le terrain est l'îlot de propriété constitué par la parcelle ou par l'ensemble des parcelles contiguës appartenant à un même propriétaire ou à une même individu)

21. DÉSIGNATION DU TERRAIN

ADRESSE DU TERRAIN (Numéro, voie, lieu-dit).   Commune   Code postal   Bureau distributeur :

NOM ET ADRESSE DU PROPRIÉTAIRE DU TERRAIN (s'il n'est pas le demandeur)

22. CADASTRE ET REMEMBREMENT

SUPERFICIE de la parcelle constituant la propriété _____ m²   Le terrain est-il inclus dans le périmètre d'une opération de REMEMBREMENT RURAL en cours de réalisation ? OUI NON   Le terrain a-t-il DÉJÀ fait l'objet d'une opération de REMEMBREMENT RURAL ? OUI NON

SECTIONS CADASTRALES, et pour chaque section le(s) numéro(s) de la ou des parcelles :

23. SITUATION JURIDIQUE DU TERRAIN

1. Le terrain est-il situé dans un lotissement ? OUI NON   NOM DU LOTISSEMENT OU DU LOTISSEUR :

NUMÉRO DU OU DES LOTS   LOTISSEMENT autorisé le   Surface hors-œuvre nette constructible sur le lot

2. Le terrain est-il situé depuis MOINS DE DIX ANS d'une plus grande propriété ? OUI NON   SI OUI, DATE D'ACQUISITION :

3. UN CERTIFICAT D'URBANISME a-t-il été délivré pour le terrain ? OUI NON   DATE DU CERTIFICAT   NUMÉRO DU CERTIFICAT   4. S'agit-il d'un terrain provenant ou la DIVISION d'une propriété bâtie ? OUI NON

24. OCCUPATION ACTUELLE DU TERRAIN

1. Existe-t-il des bâtiments sur ce terrain / obère l'atténuation, remplir la rubrique 341) OUI NON   2. Permis ces bâtiments, y en a-t-il qui sont destinés à être démolis à l'occasion de la réalisation du projet ? (Nbre l'affirmative, remplir la rubrique 242) OUI NON   Y a-t-il eu sur le terrain des bâtiments qui ont été démolis depuis le 1-4-1976 ? (Nbre l'affirmative, remplir la rubrique 243) OUI NON

DEMANDE (FACULTATIVE) D'ARRÊTÉ D'ALIGNEMENT

Aucune construction ou installation ne peut être élevée en bordure d'une voie publique sans être conforme à l'alignement.
L'arrêté d'alignement permet au demandeur de connaître avec exactitude le ou les limites actuelles ou futures du domaine public routier en bordure du terrain où repose la construction ou l'installation est envisagée. Cette demande sera transmise au(x) service(s) compétent(s) ; le ou les arrêtés d'alignement seront adressés directement au demandeur.

Je demande que ce soit délivré le ou les arrêtés d'alignement en application de l'article, 110-1 du Code de la construction et de l'habitation pour la (celles) voie(s) bordant le terrain désigné ci-dessus au cadre 2.

DATE :

SIGNATURE :

PROJET

31. ANTÉRIORITÉ

Si le projet a fait l'objet d'une demande de permis de construire antérieure, indiquer ci-contre son numéro   Cachet et signature de l'architecte ou de l'agréé en architecture

32. AUTEUR DU PROJET ARCHITECTURAL

Architecte	Agréé en architecture	Maître d'œuvre indépendant	Demandeur	Autres	QUALITÉ :

NOM, PRÉNOM et ADRESSE (dans le cas où l'auteur du projet architectural n'est pas le demandeur)

33. CARACTÉRISTIQUES DU PROJET

331. NATURE DES TRAVAUX (cocher l'une des cases indiquées de 1 à 5 puis répondre aux questions complémentaires des cas 1 à 5,6)

Construction neuve	Extension ou surélévation d'un bâtiment existant	Création de niveaux supplémentaires à l'intérieur d'un bâtiment existant	Travaux d'aménagement intérieur d'un bâtiment accompagnés d'un changement de destination des locaux	Installation de locaux dépourvus de fondations	Autres travaux
1	2	3	4	5	6

332. DESTINATION DES LOCAUX PROJETÉS

333. ASPECT EXTÉRIEUR

334. AIRES DE STATIONNEMENT

335. ESPACES VERTS

34. DENSITÉ DE LA CONSTRUCTION

NE RIEN INSCRIRE DANS LE CADRE CI-DESSOUS RÉSERVÉ À L'ADMINISTRATION

- photo-montage or sketch artist's impression of the finished job, giving both a close up and distant view of site.

The house must conform to regulations over the ratio of house to land area, the height and pitch of the roof, the position of windows in relation to neighbouring properties, and assorted other factors. As a rule of thumb, if your building will looks basically the same as its neighbours, then it will conform.

Strict planning controls help to preserve the identity of French towns – this tiled roofscape of St Emilion is typical of the Dordogne.

The *POS* sets out any special requirements in your area, e.g. the minimum distance from the house to the boundary of your land, or restrictions on the type of construction or roofing material. It also gives the *COS* (*Coefficient d'Occupation du Sol*), which sets the ratio of habitable space on your land. For example, on a plot of 1000 m² where the *COS* is 0.25, you could build a house of up to 1000 x 0.25 = 250 m². If the existing house has 150 m² you could add an extension of up to 100 m².

Other permits

If you are going to demolish any buildings to clear space, you must submit a separate *demande de permis de démolir*. If you need to cut down trees, you must submit a *demande de permis d'autorisation de coupe ou d'abattage d'arbres*.

cerfa
N° 10073-01

CADRE RÉSERVÉ À L'ADMINISTRATION

| DATE DE DÉBUT POSSIBLE DES TRAVAUX | DATE DÉPÔT | D. T | DPT | COMMUNE | ANNÉE | N° DOSSIER |

MINISTÈRE DE L'ÉQUIPEMENT, DU LOGEMENT ET DES TRANSPORTS

DÉCLARATION DE TRAVAUX EXEMPTÉS DE PERMIS DE CONSTRUIRE
OU DÉCLARATION DE CLÔTURE

1. DÉCLARANT

| NOM, PRÉNOM, ou DÉNOMINATION | NOM D'USAGE (le cas échéant) | TÉLÉPHONE |

PERSONNE MORALE (nom du REPRÉSENTANT LÉGAL ou STATUTAIRE)

| ADRESSE (numéro et voie) | COMPLÉMENT D'ADRESSE |

| CODE POSTAL | LOCALITÉ DE DESTINATION |

2. TERRAIN

21. DÉSIGNATION DU TERRAIN

| ADRESSE DU TERRAIN (numéro, voie ou lieu-dit, commune, code postal et bureau distributeur) | NOM ET ADRESSE DU PROPRIÉTAIRE DU TERRAIN (s'il est autre que le déclarant) |

22. CADASTRE

| INDIQUER LA OU LES SECTIONS CADASTRALES ET, POUR CHAQUE SECTION, LE OU LES NUMÉROS DES PARCELLES | SUPERFICIE TOTALE DE LA OU DES PARCELLES CONSTITUANT LA PROPRIÉTÉ |

23. SITUATION JURIDIQUE DU TERRAIN

| | OUI | NON | NOM DU LOTISSEMENT OU DU LOTISSEUR |
Le terrain est-il situé dans un LOTISSEMENT ?

3. PROJET

31. ANTÉRIORITÉ ÉVENTUELLE

| Si le projet a déjà fait l'objet d'une déclaration de travaux ou d'une demande de permis de construire, indiquer ci-dessous son numéro | Si le terrain a fait l'objet d'un certificat d'urbanisme, indiquer ci-dessous |
| | sa date | et | son numéro |

32. NATURE DES TRAVAUX

		FAÇADE	RAVALEMENT	AUTRE	328. NATURE ET DESCRIPTION DES TRAVAUX PROJETÉS (indiquer notamment la nature et la couleur des matériaux apparents)	CADRE RÉSERVÉ à l'administration
321.	MODIFICATION DE L'ASPECT EXTÉRIEUR D'UNE CONSTRUCTION EXISTANTE	☐	☐	☐		SUITE DONNÉE À LA DÉCLARATION
322.	CONSTRUCTION NE CRÉANT PAS DE SURFACE DE PLANCHER					
323.	CONSTRUCTION CRÉANT UNE SURFACE HORS D'ŒUVRE BRUTE N'EXCÉDANT PAS 20 M² UN TERRAIN SUPPORTANT DÉJÀ UN BÂTIMENT (ou serre de moins de 4 m de hauteur et moins de 2 000 m² de surface)					☐ opposition
324.	CONSTRUCTION OU OUVRAGE TECHNIQUE LIÉ AU FONCTIONNEMENT D'UN SERVICE PUBLIC					
325.	TRAVAUX À EXÉCUTER SUR UN IMMEUBLE CLASSÉ AU TITRE DE LA LÉGISLATION SUR LES MONUMENTS HISTORIQUES					☐ prescriptions (remplaçables ou notée)
326.	HABITATION LÉGÈRE DE LOISIRS (HLL) N'EXCÉDANT PAS 35 M²					
327.	CLÔTURE					☐ sans opposition

33. DENSITÉ DE LA CONSTRUCTION

	Surfaces hors d'œuvres brutes (SHOB)	Surfaces déduites	Surfaces hors d'œuvre nettes (SHON)
BÂTIMENT(S) EXISTANT(S)			
BÂTIMENT(S) À DÉMOLIR			
BÂTIMENT(S) À CRÉER			

4. ENGAGEMENT DU DÉCLARANT

| Je soussigné, auteur de la présente déclaration : CERTIFIE exacts les renseignements qui y sont contenus et M'ENGAGE à respecter les règles générales de construction prescrites par les textes pris en application des articles L. 111-1 et suivants du code de la construction et de l'habitation sous peine d'encourir les sanctions pénales applicables en cas de violation de ces règles (articles L. 152-1 à L. 152-11). | NOM DATE ET SIGNATURE |

DEMANDE (FACULTATIVE) D'ARRÊTÉ D'ALIGNEMENT

| Je demande que me soit délivré le ou les arrêtés d'alignement en application de l'article L. 112-1 du code de la construction et de l'habitation pour la ou les voies bordant le terrain désigné ci-dessus dans le cadre 2. | DATE ET SIGNATURE |

PC156 - Sedi UZES 30706-   327455

Un formulaire déclaration de travaux – a notice of works form. Though the form is simpler than that for a permis de construire, you need to submit almost the same detailed level of documentation with it.

The *mairie*'s architect will go through the application and may come back with alterations and requests. These must be accepted and acted on. If you haven't provided all the information that is needed, you will get a *dossier incomplet* letter, listing the further details that are required. If you haven't heard anything within two months, then you can assume that the application will be accepted. The permit should arrive in no more than three months. You must not start work without it – the penalties are heavy.

La déclaration de travaux – notice of works

This is a slightly simpler form, but must again be accompanied by plans of the site and of the building, and drawings or photomontages to illustrate the end result. In the case of a *clôture* (wall or fence), then only a site plan and sketch and description of the wall is needed.

The *mairie* has one month in which to raise any objections. This may be increased to two months if the work might fall under the scope of any outside agency – and the *mairie* will let you know if it does.

Les déclarations – notices

When you start the work, you must submit a *déclaration d'ouverture de chantier* (notice of starting work) to the *mairie*. They may send someone down, at any time, to inspect the works to check that it meets the terms of the *permis*. The *permis* or a copy of the *déclaration de travaux* must be be displayed on a panel at the front of the site. This should also give the basic information about the work, and the name of the architect or builder, as appropriate.

Within 30 days of finishing, you should send in a *déclaration d'achèvement de chantier* (notice of completion). The mairie will then send to you a *certificat de conformité* (certificate of compliance). This should arrive within three months. Keep it safely with your other house records.

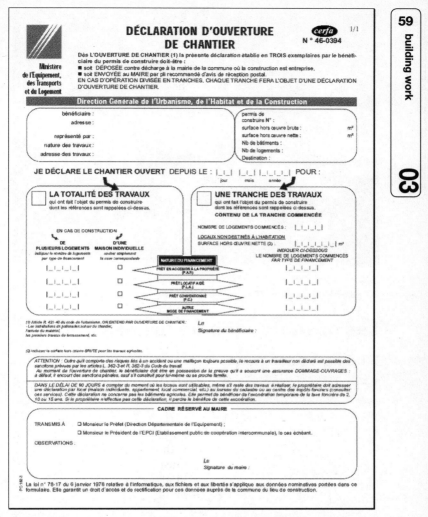

Déclaration d'ouverture de chantier – notice that 'the building site is open', i.e., work has started. When you just want to get on with the work on your house, you may find the bureaucracy a nuisance, but when you are a settled resident and keen to preserve the quality of your environment, you are more likely to appreciate the tighter controls on development. This one at least is a very simple form!

And if the paperwork starts to get you down, just remember there is usually a bar close by the mairie – there are two across the road in Miramont.

Les ouvriers – the tradesmen

Finding tradesmen

By French law, all building work has to be guaranteed for 10 years – which is good news for house owners. As part of this, the tradesmen have to carry their own 10-year insurance to cover their work, and each job also has to have insurance. (If you are organising the work yourself, you will have to arrange this.) The tradesmen also must be registered and have a *SIRET* number. This is not restricted to the building trades – all enterprises must have a number. If you don't use a *SIRET* registered builder, the work cannot be insured and will not have its 10-year guarantee. The *mairie* will have a list of *SIRET* registered tradesmen in the area.

DIY at your own risk!

If you do the work yourself or have it done by unregistered tradesmen, it will not be guaranteed and you could have problems if you wanted to sell the house later.

The informal quality checks work as well, or better, in France as in the UK especially in the rural areas. Tradesmen prefer to work in their local area, and to rely more on word of mouth than advertising for their business, so reputation is important. Ask your neighbours, or your vendors or the *immobilier* if they can recommend people for the work.

Keep an eye out for the names of builders on the notices where building is in progress. And if all else fails, France has *Pages Jaunes* (Yellow Pages) just as we do.

Le devis – the estimate

When you have found your tradesman ask for a *devis* (estimate). You should not have to pay for this. Most offer *étude et devis gratuits* (free study and estimate).

The *devis* sets the price and the specifications, and will be the finished price for the job – unless you change the specifications later. But do be clear about what you are asking for. There have been cases of people getting a *devis* for a bathroom to find that it only included equipment and delivery. If you want it *tout en place* (fitting) and *courant* (working), make sure that this is specified in the *devis*!

Le maître d'oeuvre – master of the works

A *maître d'oeuvre* is a combination of builder and architect – and normally has some training and experience in both fields. They can draw up plans, deal with the *mairie*, find tradesmen, get estimates and oversee the work for you. There is no real equivalent in the UK – the nearest is the project manager that you might find on larger sites, or the small master builder who will bring in other trades as they are needed.

A good *maître* should be able to draw on a wide knowledge of materials and techniques to suggest solutions that you would never have thought of yourself. If you want to have the work done while you are in the UK, then employing a *maître* is an obvious solution even for the simpler jobs. Even if you are there yourself, employing a *maître* should ensure that the job is done better, and the extra cost may not be that much in the long run.

Other trades

- *maçon* – builder, general term
- *charpentier* – carpenter, specialising in roof timbers
- *couvreur* – roofer, working with tiles, slates or similar.
- *électricien* – electrician
- *menuisier* – joiner, for windows, doors, etc.
- *plâtrier* – plasterer
- *plombier* – plumber

We will meet these and other tradesmen in the rest of the book.

Lexicon: les travaux – building work

architecte conseil	consultant architect employed by the DDE
certificat de conformité	certificate of compliance
chantier (m)	building site
COS (Coefficient d'Occupation du Sol)	– the maximum permissible ratio of floor space to land area
DDE (Direction Départementale de l'Equipement)	– the département's planning authority
déclaration...	notice...
... d'achèvement de chantier	... of completion
... d'ouverture de chantier	... of starting work
... de travaux	... of works
devis (m)	estimate
devis gratuit	free estimate
formulaire (m)	form
maçon (m)	builder, general term
maire (m)	mayor
maître d'oeuvre	master of the works, project manager for building work
ouvrier (m)	tradesman

permis... | permit...
... de construire | ... to build
... de démolir | ... to demolish a building
... d'autorisation de coupe ou d'abattage d'arbres | ... of authorisation to cut down trees
POS (Plan d'Occupation du Sol) | planning brief for land use in commune

English–French quick reference

architect | architecte
builder | maçon (m)
building site | chantier (m)
consultant architect | architecte conseil
certificate of compliance | certificat de conformité
estimate | devis (m)
form | formulaire (m)
land use brief | POS (Plan d'Occupation du Sol)
mayor | maire (m)
master of the works | maître d'oeuvre
notice... | déclaration...
... of completion | ... d'achèvement de chantier
... of starting work | ... d'ouverture de chantier
... of works | ... de travaux
permit... | permis...
... to build | ... de construire
... to demolish a building | ... de demolir
... to cut down trees | ... d'autorisation de coupe ou d'abattage d'arbres
tradesman | ouvrier (m)

04

la structure –
the structure

Almost the same...

The French seem to be very keen on preserving regional identities in their housing. This is less so in the larger towns and cities, but in smaller places – especially in the more picturesque areas – the houses typically all have the same look. Red tiled roofs throughout the South, over the white walls of houses packed close together on hills in Provence, but over pastel walls of houses in the fields of the Dordogne; over *colombage* (half-timbered) walls and plain wood shutters in the south west. In Britanny, sturdy slates or thick thatches and tough granite walls protect against the weather that blows in from the North Atlantic, while across on the borders with Switzerland, broad roofs overhang the balconies around wooden chalets.

And the regional look is often not just a matter of preference. We have listed buildings and preservation areas in the UK, and so do the French. But they go further. The French believe that, though the house may belong to you, its external appearance is a matter of common concern. If you plan to build a new house, or make changes to an existing one, and want yours to stand out from its neighbours, think again. You can have your individuality, but it must be within the limits of the regional look.

On a purely practical level, all old French houses – and many new ones – have solid walls. Cavity walls are not standard, as they are in the UK. The walls of new houses are often built of hollow red bricks, which are large and light and go up very quickly. With rendering on the outside and insulated plasterboard on the inside, these have reasonable insulating qualities.

Check at the mairie

- If you are planning any change to the outside of the house, talk to the planning officer at the *mairie* at an early stage – see Chapter 3.

- The *mairie* should have a list of registered tradesmen in your area.

La structure – the structure

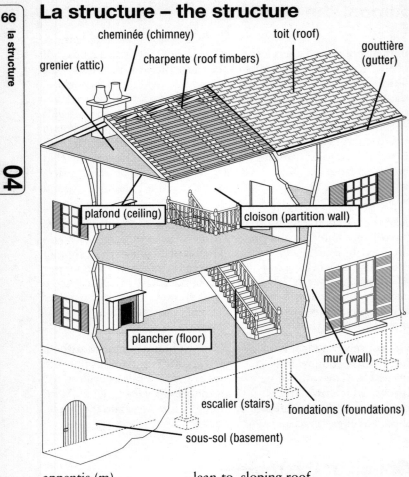

grenier (attic)

cheminée (chimney)

charpente (roof timbers)

toit (roof)

gouttière (gutter)

plafond (ceiling)

cloison (partition wall)

plancher (floor)

mur (wall)

escalier (stairs)

fondations (foundations)

sous-sol (basement)

appentis (m)	lean-to, sloping roof
bois de charpente (m)	roof timbers or more simply…
charpente (m)	roof timbers
cheminée (f)	chimney
cloison (f)	partition wall
détritus (m)	rubbish
escalier (m)	stairs
fondations (f)	foundations – often absent from older houses

fouille (f)	the act of digging foundations
gravats (m)	rubble
grenier (m)	attic/loft
moisi (m)	mould
moisissure (f)	mildew
mur (m)	wall
mur mitoyen	party wall
plafond (m)	ceiling
plancher (m)	floor
pourriture (f)	rot
puits (m) de jour	light shaft – skylight over a stairwell or inner room, to allow in daylight
sous-sol	basement
toit (m)	roof

La toiture – the roofing

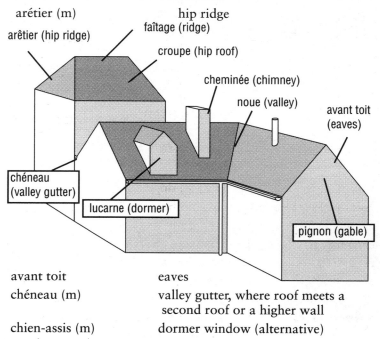

arétier (m)   hip ridge
arêtier (hip ridge) faîtage (ridge)
                     croupe (hip roof)
                     cheminée (chimney)
                     noue (valley)
                     avant toit (eaves)
chéneau (valley gutter)
lucarne (dormer)
pignon (gable)

avant toit	eaves
chéneau (m)	valley gutter, where roof meets a second roof or a higher wall
chien-assis (m)	dormer window (alternative)

croupe (f)	hip roof
écran de sous-toiture	lining felt
faîtage (f)	ridge
fronton (m)	pediment (wall higher than the end of the roof)
lucarne (f)	dormer window
noue (f)	valley (inner angle where two roofs meet)
planches de rive (f)	eaves fascia (board beneath eaves)
pignon (m)	gable end
planche (f) de rives	eaves board or fascia
solin (m)	flashing
toiture-terrasse (f)	terrace roof
vélux (m)	(Velux) skylight

vélux

Le bois de charpente – the roof timbers

You will hear the roof timbers called *les combles, le bois de charpente* and sometimes *la charpente*.

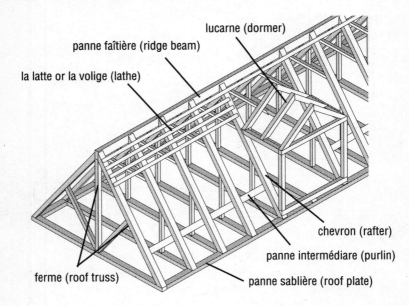

lucarne (dormer)

panne faîtière (ridge beam)

la latte or la volige (lathe)

chevron (rafter)

panne intermédiare (purlin)

ferme (roof truss)

panne sablière (roof plate)

In older houses and house with gables, the roof will normally be made from rafters on a ridge beam and wall plates, braced by horizontal beams. In other cases, ready-made triangular trusses will be used to create the basic structure.

arbalétrier (m)	rafter as part of truss
armature à toit	roof truss
chêne	oak
chevron (m)	rafter
ferme (f)	roof truss
fermette (f)	small trusses, factory-made
latte (f)	lathes
lattis (m)	lathing – all the lathes as a set
liteau (m)	batten
lucarne	dormer
panne (f)	horizontal beam
panne faîtière	ridge beam
panne intermédiare	purlin (horizontal tie on rafters)
panne sablière	roof plate, resting on top of walls
pin (m)	pine
poutre (f)	beam
rampart (m)	roof arch
voligeage (m)	the act of putting lathes in place
xylophène (m)	wood preservative

An attic with ramparts (arches), like this one, will be easier to convert into a habitable room, than one where the roof is formed from trusses

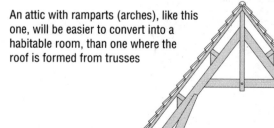

Lathes and tiles

If the roof is to be covered with slates or flat
tiles, these will be hung on lathes. Lathes are
also used now with curved tiles, but on
older houses you may find flat planking
or triangular supports (see illustration).
The tiles are sometimes simply placed
on top of these – not attached – and
have a tendency to slip steadily down
the roof over the years.

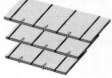

As in the UK, you will not find lining felt under the tiles of older
houses, unless they have been reroofed recently.

> If the immobilier's advert says toiture en bon état, all that
> means is that it doesn't leak – much.

La couverture – roofing materials

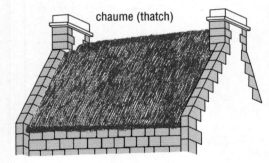

chaume (thatch)

ardoise (slates)

la plaque profilée en fibro-
ciment (roofing panels in
fibre-cement)

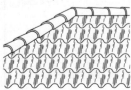

bardeaux bitumés
(bitumen shingles)

tuile en terre cuite
(clay tiles)

ardoise (f)	slate
bardeau de bitume	bitumen shingles, used instead of or to replace slates, laid on a fully planked roof
bardeau (m) de bois	wood shingle
chaume (m)	thatch
crochet (m) inox	stainless steel slate clip
feutre à toit	roofing felt
génoise (f)	eaves for curved tile roof, made out of layers of tiles
plaque (f) profilée	roofing panel, sometimes placed beneath curved tiles to ensure weatherproof roof
terre cuite	clay
tuile (f)	tile
tuile canal/romane	curved tile
tuile plate	flat tile

Génoise eaves

roof tiles

flat tile layer

two layers of curved tiles

wall

A roof in Gironde with génoise eaves – though these are not the standard curved tiles, and notice the glass tiles used to let light into the attic.

Roofing tradesmen

- If you want to build, adapt or mend the roofing timbers, you need a *charpentier* – (think 'carpenter').

- If you need to replace or mend a roof, you need un *couvreur* (a roofer). And if it's a thatched roof, make sure that he is *un couvreur de toits de chaume* (a roofer of roofs of thatch).

Les murs – walls

Walls start from foundations (though not necessarily). In older houses, especially in country areas and where large stones were the building material, the walls were often built directly on the ground. Two possible problems can arise from this. You can get subsidence, though with an old house it's a reasonable bet that it has sunk as much as it's going to. You may also have rising damp, as there wil be no barrier beneath the stones. The damp problem will be worse if the original – breathing – floor of beaten earth or flagstones has been replaced by concrete and tiles.

Les fondations – foundations

barrière d'étanchéité (f)	damp course
blocaille (f)	hardcore
fissures (f)	cracks
fondations (f)	foundations
humidité (f)	damp
infiltration (f)	rising damp
jointoyer	point – renew mortar of walls
maçonnage (m)	building
mur (m)	wall
tranchée (f)	trench
terrassement (m)	excavation

External walls

For new building, the French favour hollow concrete or clay blocks (*briques*). These come in a wide range of sizes and cross-sections, offering different weight to strength ratios. The resulting walls are not very attractive when bare, but they are not intended to remain bare. The outside is normally rendered with mortar, or sometimes clad with *bardage* (weatherboarding). The inside is either rendered or lined with plasterboard.

Where a wall is built with a cavity, the structure is usually different from in the UK. Here a cavity wall has an inner load-bearing skin of brick or breeze block, and an outer skin of brick. In France the cavity is formed by adding a thin inner skin to a standard thickness, load-bearing outer wall. Both inner and outer walls are often made of hollow bricks.

Some wall styles

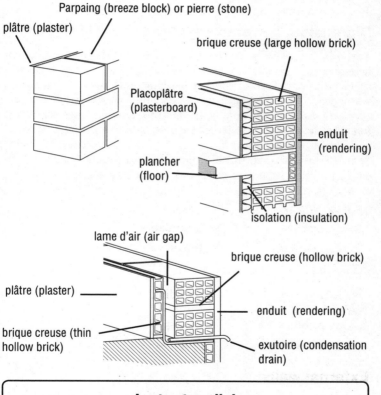

Parpaing (breeze block) or pierre (stone)

plâtre (plaster)

brique creuse (large hollow brick)

Placoplâtre (plasterboard)

enduit (rendering)

plancher (floor)

isolation (insulation)

lame d'air (air gap)

brique creuse (hollow brick)

plâtre (plaster)

enduit (rendering)

brique creuse (thin hollow brick)

exutoire (condensation drain)

Instant walls!

If you want a very strong, solid wall quickly, build a dry wall – no mortar – of the hollowest bricks, slide reinforcing rods down through them, then fill with wet concrete.

Les cloisons and parois – partition walls

Some or all of the internal walls of a house will be *cloisons* – partitions. Smaller farms and terraced houses in towns are often built with the floor and ceiling joists supported solely by the outside walls. Keep this in mind when you look around old houses. *Cloisons* are easily removed and rebuilt elsewhere if you want to remodel the internal layout.

Old *cloisons* are likely to be lathe and plaster or thin, solid brick. New ones are quickly built from thin hollow bricks, plasterboard on wooden frames or plaster blocks.

Digression: carreaux de plâtre – plaster blocks

You won't find these in the UK, but plaster blocks are worth investigating. They are typically 66 × 50 cm, in widths from 5 to 12 cm and come in different weights and finishes – including waterproof ones for bathrooms and lightweight ones for loft conversions. They are not cheap, and the standard ones are heavy, but they slot and stick together easily, can be cut with a wood saw and need no framework. Exposed corners can be reinforced with an angled metal strip, if required. After a little fine filling of the ends and joints, the new wall is ready for decorating.

Wall materials

agglo (m)	breeze block
ancre de mur (m)	wall tie
béton (m)	concrete
béton armé	reinforced concrete
brique (f)	brick
brique creuse	hollow brick
brique réfractaire	firebrick
calcaire (m)	limestone
carreau de plâtre	plaster block
ciment (m)	cement
colombage (m)	half-timbered
cornière (f)	angled strip for reinforcing corner of plaster wall

crépi	roughcast – external wall covering applied like plaster, or sprayed from a machine
doublage	lining – could be plasterboard
enduit (m)	rendering
granit (m)	granite
grès (m)	sandstone
isolation (f)	insulation
lame d'air (f)	air gap – may contain insulation
linteau (m)	lintel
moellon (m)	quarry stone
mortier (m)	mortar
panneau (m)	panel
panneau de particule	chipboard panel
parpaing (m)	breeze block
pierre (f)	stone
pierre de taille	dressed stone
placoplâtre (m)	plasterboard
torchis (m)	wattle and daub – a mixture of clay, straw and other substances on a framework of woven sticks
sable (m)	sand
sable gris	coarse sand

Isolation – insulation

bourrelet en caoutchouc	rubber beading
calfeutrage (m)	draught-proofing
fibres de verre	fibreglass
joint d'étanchéité (m)	draught excluder
joint en mousse (m)	foam strip
laine (f) de roche	rockwool
liège en particules (m)	cork particles
panneau isolant (m)	insulation panel
plaque complexe (f)	composite panel – e.g. plasterboard backed with an insulating material
plaque isolante (f)	insulation panel

polystyrène (m)   polystyrene
polyuréthane (m)   polyurethane
vermiculite (f)   mica particles

Building tradesmen

- ◆ A builder is a *maçon*, whatever material he uses.
- ◆ If you want a stonemason, ask for a *tailleur*.
- ◆ For plastering, you need a *plâtrier*.

Les outils de maçon – builder's tools

Brickwork

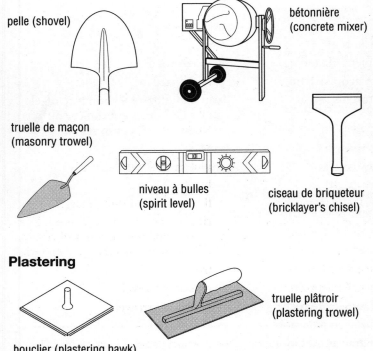

pelle (shovel)

bétonnière
(concrete mixer)

truelle de maçon
(masonry trowel)

niveau à bulles
(spirit level)

ciseau de briqueteur
(bricklayer's chisel)

Plastering

truelle plâtroir
(plastering trowel)

bouclier (plastering hawk)

seau (bucket)

truelle (trowel)

taloche
(float)

grattoir
(shavehook)

couteau à enduire
(filling knife)

bêche (f)	spade
bétonnière (f)	concrete mixer
bouclier (m)	plastering hawk
ciseau (m)	chisel
ciseau de briqueteur	bricklayer's chisel
ciseau de maçon	mason's chisel
couteau à enduire	filling knife
gâche (f)	plastering trowel
grattoir	shavehook (triangular scraper)
niveau à bulles	spirit level
pelle (f)	shovel
pioche (f)	pick
plâtroir (m)	plastering trowel
seau (m)	bucket
taloche (f)	float, for smoothing plaster
tamis (m)	riddle – box with a fine mesh base for removing lumps and stones from sand or other dry material
truelle (f)	trowel
truelle de maçon	masonry trowel
truelle plâtroir	plastering trowel

Sometimes there are several words for the same thing. Try
to learn one well enough to be able to ask for it, and others
well enough to recognise them when you hear them.

Les plafonds et les planchers – ceilings and floors

In older houses, the ceiling and floor are often – literally – two sides of the same thing! The traditional wooden floor consists of planks laid over joists, and the undersides of the planks form the ceiling. In houses without central heating, this allows the warmth from the downstairs living rooms to rise up to the bedrooms – but it also lets the noise up.

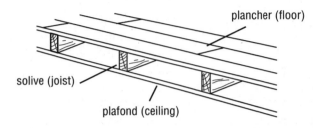

plancher (floor)

solive (joist)

plafond (ceiling)

If there is a ceiling, it will be made of thin wood pannelling (*le lambris*) or, as in the UK, of lathe and plaster (*en lattes et enduit de plâtre*) or plasterboard (*placoplâtre*).

In apartments and in more modern houses, the floor may be made of reinforced concrete. Apart from better sound-proofing, this also allows the use of ceramic tiles for floors in upstairs rooms. (You cannot lay hard tiles on flexible wood floors.)

plancher (m)	floor
solive (f)	joist
plafond (m)	ceiling
lambris (m)	pannelling
lattes et enduit de plâtre	lathe and plaster

English–French quick reference

The structure – la structure

attic	grenier (m)
basement	sous-sol
ceiling	plafond (m)
chimney	cheminée (f)
floor	plancher (m)
foundations	fondations (f)
lean-to	appentis (m)
mould	moisi (m) or moisissure (f)
party wall	mur mitoyen
porch	porche (m)
rot	pourriture (f)
rubbish	détritus (m)
rubble	gravats (m)
stairs	escalier (m)
wall	mur (m)

Roofing – la toiture

attic	grenier (m)
beam	panne (f), poutre (f)
carpenter, for roof	charpentier (m)
ceiling	plafond (m)
chimney	cheminée (f)
clay	terre cuite
dormer window	lucarne (f)
dormer window	chien-assis (m)
eaves	rive (f), avant toit
flashing	solin (m)
gable	pignon (m)
hip ridge	arétier (m)
hip roof	croupe (f)

lathe	latte (f), volige (f)
lining felt	écran de sous-toiture
oak	chêne
pediment	fronton (m)
pine	pin (m)
rafter	chevron (m)
ridge	faîtage (m)
roof	toit (m)
roof timbers	bois de charpente (m)
roof truss	ferme (f), fermette (f), armature à toit
roofer	couvreur (m)
roofing felt	feutre à toit
roofing panel	plaque (f) profilée
shingle	bardeau (m) de bois, de bitume
skylight	vélux (m)
slate	ardoise (f)
slate clip	crochet (m)
sloping roof	appentis (m)
terrace roof	toiture-terrasse (f)
thatch	chaume (m)
tile	tuile (f)
tile, curved	tuile canal/romane
valley	noue (f)
valley gutter	chéneau (m)
wood preservative	xylophène (m)

Walls – les murs

air gap	lame d'air (f)
breeze block	parpaing (m), agglo (m)
brick	brique (f)
brick, hollow	brique creuse
builder	maçon (m)
building (work)	maçonnage (f)

cement	ciment (m)
chipboard	panneau (m) de particule
concrete	béton (m)
concrete, reinforced	béton armé
crack (in wall)	fissure (f)
damp	humidité (f)
damp course	barrière d'étanchéité (f)
excavation	terrassement (m)
floor	plancher (m)
foundations	fondations (f)
granite	granit (m)
half-timbered	colombage (m)
insulation	isolation (f)
limestone	calcaire (m)
lining (for wall)	doublage (m)
lintel	linteau (m)
mildew	moisissure (f)
mortar	mortier (m)
mould	moisi (m)
panel	panneau (m), plaque (f)
partition wall	cloison (f)
plaster	plâtre (m)
plaster block	carreau de plâtre
plasterboard	placoplâtre (m)
plasterer	plâtrier (m)
point (walls)	jointoyer
quarry stone	moellon (m)
rendering	enduit (m)
rising damp	infiltration (f)
rot	pourriture (f)
roughcast	crépi (m)
rubbish	détritus (m)
rubble	gravats (m)
sand	sable (m)

sandstone	grès (m)
stone	pierre (f)
stone, dressed	pierre de taille
stonemason	tailleur (m)
trench	tranchée (f)
wall	mur (m)
wall tie	ancre de mur (f)
wattle and daub	torchis (m)

Tools – les outils

bricklayer's chisel	ciseau de briqueteur
bucket	seau (m)
chisel	ciseau (m)
concrete mixer	bétonnière (f)
filling knife	couteau à enduire
float	taloche (f)
pick	pioche (m)
plastering hawk	bouclier (m)
plastering trowel	plâtroir (m), gâche (f)
riddle	tamis (m)
shavehook	grattoir (m)
shovel	pelle (f)
spade	bêche (f)
spirit level	niveau à bulles
trowel	truelle (f)

Ceilings and floors – plafonds et planchers

ceiling	plafond (m)
floor	plancher (m)
joist	solive (f)
lathe and plaster	lattes et enduit de plâtre
pannelling	lambris (m)

05

la menuiserie
— woodwork

Almost the same...

In the UK, building professionals make a distinction between joinery or carpentry, though for most of us, it's all woodwork. The French make a similar distinction. If you want someone to make, fit or mend fit staircases, windows, doors and the like, you need *un menuisier*.

The most obvious difference is in the windows. Most French houses – virtually all of them south of the Loire – have shutters. I'm a fan of shutters. They keep the sun out on a summer's day, the warmth in on a winter's night, and the burglars out when you're away. A side effect of having shutters is that the windows must open inwards. (You can get windows that open outwards. They are said to be *à l'anglaise*.)

There's a small but significant difference in the way they hang doors – they use split hinges. I'm a fan of these too, and so will you be the next time that you are painting a door, laying floor tiles, moving big furniture or doing any other job where a door in a doorway is a nuisance. With split hinges, you just lift the door off and prop it up somewhere out of the way.

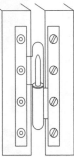

Split hinges make a simple job of hanging (and unhanging) doors – as long as you fit them the right way up!

Check at the mairie

◆ Your internal fittings are entirely your affair, but if you are adding or altering external doors or windows – especially on the publicly-visible sides of the house – check with the *mairie* if the new ones are different from the others in the neighbourhood.

Off the shelf but customised

Lapeyre, one of the biggest DIY suppliers, offers a customising service for replacement shutters, windows and doors. Lift the old one off its hinges and take it to the nearest store, and they will trim a ready-made one to fit. Very handy!

Les menuiseries intérieures – internal woodwork

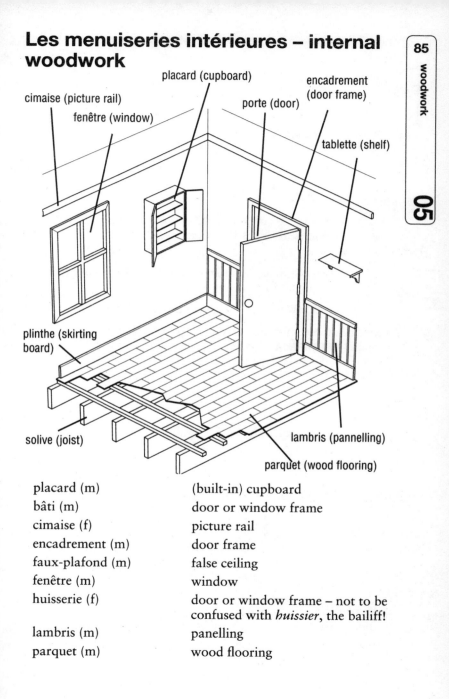

placard (cupboard)

cimaise (picture rail)

fenêtre (window)

porte (door)

encadrement (door frame)

tablette (shelf)

plinthe (skirting board)

solive (joist)

lambris (pannelling)

parquet (wood flooring)

placard (m)	(built-in) cupboard
bâti (m)	door or window frame
cimaise (f)	picture rail
encadrement (m)	door frame
faux-plafond (m)	false ceiling
fenêtre (m)	window
huisserie (f)	door or window frame – not to be confused with *huissier*, the bailiff!
lambris (m)	panelling
parquet (m)	wood flooring

placard (m)	built-in cupboard
planche (f)	floorboard
plancher (m)	floor
plinthe (f)	skirting board
porte (f)	door
solive (f)	joist
tablette (f)	shelf

Les portes – doors

Apart from the use of split hinges for hanging, the thing to note with French doors is that that are sold ready-made in two forms:

- *Un bloc porte* (door block) consists of the door and its frame with the hinges and lock fitted.

- *Une porte seule* (door alone) is just the door.

External doors may be offered as part of a complete set with matching fixed lights, glazed side panels and gap fillers.

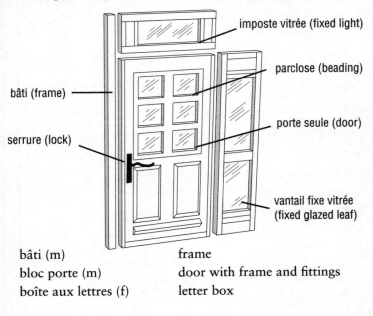

imposte vitrée (fixed light)

parclose (beading)

bâti (frame)

porte seule (door)

serrure (lock)

vantail fixe vitrée (fixed glazed leaf)

bâti (m)	frame
bloc porte (m)	door with frame and fittings
boîte aux lettres (f)	letter box

bouton (de porte)	door knob
chambranle (m)	door frame
encadrement (m)	architrave, door frame
imposte vitrée (f)	fanlight
parclose (m)	beading for fixing glass
porte (f)	door
porte blindée	high-security (armoured) door
porte coulissante	sliding door
porte va et vient	swing door
seuil (m)	doorstep, sill
vantail fixe vitré (m)	fixed glazed leaf

Quincaillerie pour les portes – hardware for doors

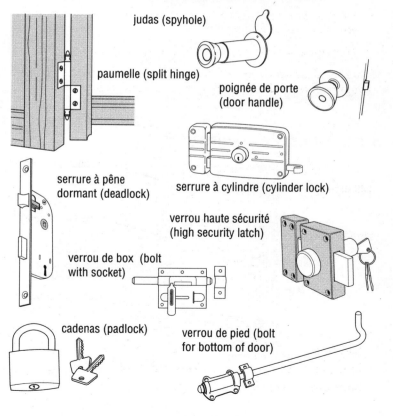

judas (spyhole)

paumelle (split hinge)

poignée de porte
(door handle)

serrure à pêne
dormant (deadlock)

serrure à cylindre (cylinder lock)

verrou haute sécurité
(high security latch)

verrou de box (bolt
with socket)

cadenas (padlock)

verrou de pied (bolt
for bottom of door)

cadenas (m)	padlock
charnière (f)	hinge
clé (f)	key
fermeture (f)	catch, also means closing of doors
gâche (f)	striking plate of lock
judas (m)	spyhole for door
paumelle (f)	split hinge
penture (f) anglaise	English hinge – standard UK style
poignée (f) de porte	door handle
serrure (f) encastrée	mortice lock
serrure à cylindre	cylinder lock
serrure à pêne dormant	deadlock
trou (m) de serrure	keyhole
verrou (m)	bolt
verrou de box	bolt with socket
verrou de pied	long bolt for bottom of door
verrou haute sécurité	high security latch
verrou pistolet	bolt to fit into frame

Les fenêtres – windows

Traditionally, windows are hinged and deep-set, and either open outward – a style known as *à l'anglaise* – or, where there are shutters, open inwards – *à la française*.

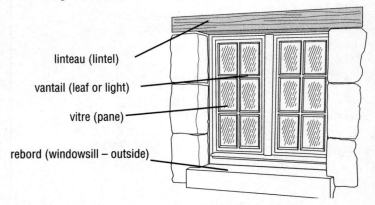

linteau (lintel)

vantail (leaf or light)

vitre (pane)

rebord (windowsill – outside)

Other opening styles include:

- *soufflet*   hinged at the bottom, opening in and down
- *basculant*   swivelling horizontally
- *coulissant*   sliding

à l'anglaise

à la française

soufflet

coulissant

basculant

La fenêtre – the window

appui (m)	windowsill – inside
carreau (m) de fenêtre	window pane
châssis (m)	window frame
double vitrage	double glazing
fenêtre à battants	casement window
fenêtre à croisillons	lattice window
fenêtre à guillotine	sash window
fenêtre en saillie	bay window
fenêtre à tabatière	skylight
linteau (m)	lintel
oeil-de-boeuf (m)	ox-eye window– small round window in attic
porte-fenêtre (f)	french window
rebord (m)	windowsill – outside
vantail (m)	leaf or light
verre (m)	glass
vitrage (m)	glazing
vitre (f)	pane

Les volets – shutters

Shutters are fitted on doors and windows to give extra security, shade and insulation. There are many styles – in wood and other materials. In this small book we only have room to cover a few of the more popular.

Les volets battants

Battant means that the shutters are hinged and open flat against the outside wall, where they are held by a *tourniquet* or *tête de berger* (shutter catch). To secure the shutters when closed, they normally use an *espagnolette* – a rod that holds the two leaves together and locks into the top and bottom of the frame. There are three main styles of *volets battants*.

Le volet penture

Made from tongue and grooved wood, held together by strap hinges.

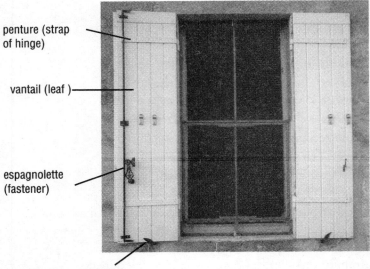

penture (strap of hinge)

vantail (leaf)

espagnolette (fastener)

tourniquet (shutter catch)

Un volet penture on a Gironde ferme – the screen over the window is a moustiquaire (mosquito screen) – very useful if the house is near water.

Le volet barres

Also made from tongue and grooved wood, this is held together by cross pieces – if there is a diagonal brace, it is *un volet barres et écharpe*.

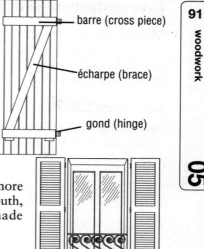

barre (cross piece)

écharpe (brace)

gond (hinge)

Le volet persienne

Made from slats in a frame – a more common design as you get further south, these provide ventilation and shade rather than insulation and shade.

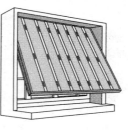

La persienne

Not to be confused with *volets persiennes*, the *persiennes* are also slatted, but open differently and only seen on windows – not on doors. Some *persiennes* are hinged to open upwards, others fold concertina-style against the sides of the window frame. Some can be folded either way.

Le volet roulant

These are made from PVC or metal, not wood, but I'm going to put them here anyway! Roller shutters can be fitted inside the door or window frame, or project out from it. They can be hand-wound or electrically operated.

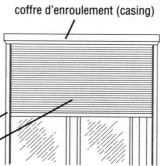

coffre d'enroulement (casing)

coulisse (tracking)

tablier de lames (shutter of strips)

Quincaillerie pour les volets – hardware for shutters

tourniquet (shutter catch)

tête de bergère (shutter catch)

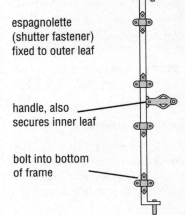

espagnolette
(shutter fastener)
fixed to outer leaf

handle, also
secures inner leaf

bolt into bottom
of frame

Les volets

coffre d'enroulement (m)	casing for roller shutter
coulisse (f)	tracking on roller shutters
crémone (f)	window lock
écharpe (f)	diagonal brace on shutter
espagnolette (f)	shutter fastening
gond (m)	hinge
loquet (m)	latch
penture (f)	strap of hinge
persienne (f)	slatted shutter
tête de bergère (f)	shepherdess's head shutter catch
tablier de lames (m)	shutter of strips
tourniquet (m)	shutter catch
vantail (m)	leaf, single shutter
volet barre (m)	wooden shutter with cross bars
volet pentures	shutter with strap hinges
volet persienne	slatted shutter
volet roulant	roller shutters

Les escaliers – staircases

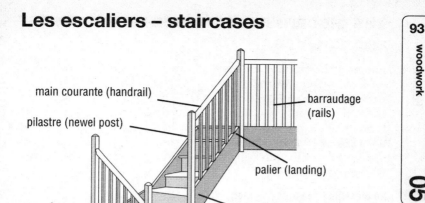

main courante (handrail)

pilastre (newel post)

barraudage (rails)

palier (landing)

limon (string board)

marche (step)

volée (flight)

contre-marche (riser)

barraudage (m)	rails
contre-marche (f)	riser
échelle (f)	ladder
escabeau (m)	step ladder
escalier (m)	staircase
escalier en colimaçon	spiral staircase
escalier escamotable	fold-away stairs, e.g. for loft
escalier spiral	spiral staircase
giron (m)	width of step
limon (m)	string board – plank that supports steps
main courante (f)	handrail
marche (f)	step
palier (f)	landing
pilastre (m)	pilaster, newel post
volée (f)	flight

Les placards et étagères – cupboards and shelves

For most of us, making built-in cupboards and shelves isn't a *menuiserie* job – we just head for the nearest IKEA and buy flat-packs and shelving systems. It's the same in France. You'll find IKEA there, but if you want proper French style, shop with the locals like Camif and Lapeyre. You could, for example, kit out your *chambre de maître* (master bedroom) with a fully equipped *dressing* (literally, 'dressing room' but in practice it will usually be a fitted wardrobe).

Le dressing – the dressing room
(Typical elements in a flat-pack kit)

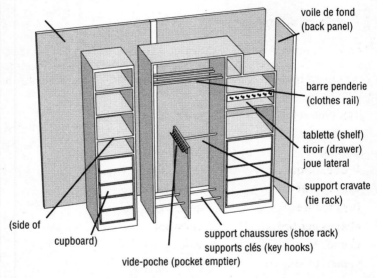

voile de fond (back panel)

barre penderie (clothes rail)

tablette (shelf)
tiroir (drawer)
joue lateral

support cravate (tie rack)

(side of cupboard)

support chaussures (shoe rack)
supports clés (key hooks)

vide-poche (pocket emptier)

armoire (f)	wardrobe
barre penderie	clothes rail
dressing (m)	dressing room/fitted wardrobe
dressing d'angle	wardrobe fitted in corner
en niche	in an alcove
étagère (f)	shelf
joue lateral (f)	side of cupboard

portes coulissantes	sliding doors
portes pliantes	folding doors
rayonnage (m)	set of shelves
support chaussures	shoe rack
support (m) clé	key hook
support (m) chaussures	shoe rack
support (m) cravate	tie rack
tablette (f)	shelf
tiroir (m)	drawer
vide-poche (m)	pocket emptier
voile de fond	back panel

Le bois – wood

The wood section of a French *bricolage* looks much the same as one in any UK DIY store. Don't get misled by the term *massif*. *Bois massif* is solid wood – of any size – as opposed to some form of *panneau* (manufactured panel).

aggloméré (m)	chipboard
baguette (f)	beading
bois dur	hardwood
bois exotique	tropical hardwood
bois massif	solid wood
bois tendre	softwood
châtaigner (m)	chestnut
chêne (m)	oak
contre-plaqué (m)	plywood
contre-plaqué replaqué	plywood with veneer
hêtre (m)	beech
médium	MDF (medium density fibreboard)
mélaminé	melamine-coated
panneau (m) de bois	wood panel
panneau de fibres dures	hardboard
panneau mélaminé	melamine surfaced chipboard panel, e.g. Contiboard

panneau plaqué	veneered chipboard panel
placage (m)	veneer
à rainure et languette	tongue and grooved
sapin (m)	pine
sapin du nord (SPN)	Scandinavian pine

Les outils – tools

If you are going to do any *bricolage* (DIY), you will need *des outils* (some tools) and *une boîte à outils* (a toolbox) – or even *un atelier* (a workshop) – to keep them in. Here's an assortment of tools that you may find useful.

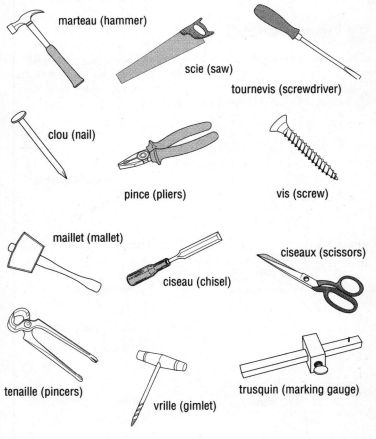

marteau (hammer)

scie (saw)

tournevis (screwdriver)

clou (nail)

pince (pliers)

vis (screw)

maillet (mallet)

ciseau (chisel)

ciseaux (scissors)

tenaille (pincers)

vrille (gimlet)

trusquin (marking gauge)

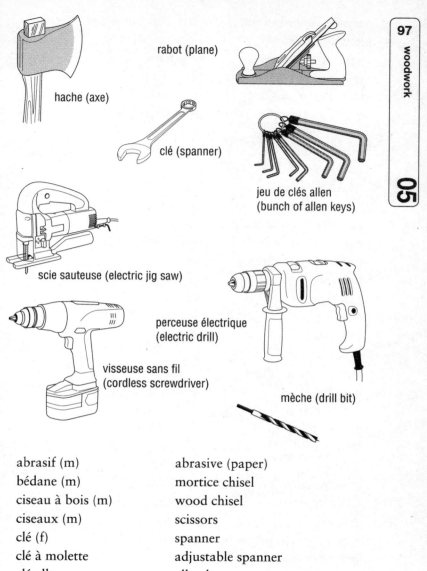

hache (axe)

rabot (plane)

clé (spanner)

jeu de clés allen
(bunch of allen keys)

scie sauteuse (electric jig saw)

perceuse électrique
(electric drill)

visseuse sans fil
(cordless screwdriver)

mèche (drill bit)

abrasif (m)	abrasive (paper)
bédane (m)	mortice chisel
ciseau à bois (m)	wood chisel
ciseaux (m)	scissors
clé (f)	spanner
clé à molette	adjustable spanner
clé allen	allen key
clou (m)	nail
colle à bois	wood glue
coupe-verre (m)	glass cutter

couteau universel (m)	cutter (Stanley knife)
double équerre	T-square
équerre (f) droite	set square
fausse équerre	bevel square
forte agrafeuse (f)	staple gun
jeu de clés	set of spanners
maillet (m)	mallet
marteau (m)	hammer
mèche (f)	drill bit
mètre (m) pliant	folding rule
mètre à ruban	tape measure
paire (f) de ciseaux	scissors
papier (m) de verre	sandpaper
perceuse (f) électrique	electric drill
pince (f)	pliers
poinçon (m)	bradawl
ponceuse (f)	sander
rabot (m)	plane
râpe (f)	rasp
réglet (m) métallique	metal rule
scie (f)	saw
scie circulaire	circular saw
scie sauteuse	electric jig saw
tenaille (f)	pincers
tournevis (m)	screwdriver
trusquin (m)	mortice gauge
vilebrequin (m)	brace, of bit and brace
vis (f)	screw
visseuse (f) électrique	electric screwdriver
vrille (f)	gimlet

English–French quick reference

Internal woodwork – les menuiseries intérieures

cupboard	armoire (f) or placard (m)
false ceiling	faux-plafond (m)
floor	plancher (m)
floorboard	planche (f)
frame, door or window	bâti (m) or huisserie (f)
joist	solive (f)
panelling	lambris (m)
picture rail	cimaise (f)
shelf	tablette (f)
skirting board	plinthe (f)
wood flooring	parquet (m)

Doors – les portes

architrave	encadrement (m)
beading for glass	parclose (m)
door	porte (f)
door frame	bâti (m) or chambranle (m)
door knob	bouton (de porte)
doorstep	seuil (m)
fanlight	imposte vitrée (f)
letter box	boîte (f) aux lettres
sliding door	porte coulissante
swing door	porte va et vient

Hardware for doors – quincaillerie pour les portes

bolt	verrou (m)
catch	fermeture (f)
cylinder lock	serrure à cylindre
deadlock	serrure à pêne dormant
door handle	poignée (f) de porte
hinge	charnière (f)

hinge, English	penture (f) anglaise
hinge, split	paumelle (f)
key	clé (f)
keyhole	trou (m) de serrure
mortice lock	serrure (f) encastrée
spyhole for door	judas (m)

Windows – les fenêtres

bay window	fenêtre en saillie
casement window	fenêtre à battants
double glazing	double vitrage
french window	porte-fenêtre (f)
glass	verre (m)
leaf or light	vantail (m)
lintel	linteau (m)
pane	vitre (f)
sash window	fenêtre à guillotine
skylight	fenêtre à tabatière
window frame	châssis (m)
window pane	carreau (m) de fenêtre
windowsill – inside	appui (m)
windowsill – outside	rebord (m)

Shutters – les volets

hinge	gond (m)
latch	loquet (m)
roller shutter	volet roulant
roller shutter, casing	coffre d'enroulement (m)
shutter catch	tête bergère (f) or tourniquet (m)
shutter fastening	espagnolette (f)
shutter, slatted	persienne (f)
shutter with cross bars	volet barre
shutter with slats	volet persienne
shutter with strap hinges	volet pentures

| strap hinge | penture (f) |
| window lock | crémone (f) |

Staircases – les escaliers

ladder	échelle (f)
flight of steps	volée (f)
fold-away stairs	escalier escamotable
landing	palier (m)
handrail	main courante (f)
newel post	pilastre (m)
rails	barraudage (m)
riser	contre-marche (f)
spiral staircase	escalier en colimaçon, or spiral
staircase	escalier (m)
step	marche (f)
step ladder	escabeau (m)

Cupboards and shelves – les placards et les étagères

clothes rail	barre penderie
drawer	tiroir (m)
doors, folding	portes pliantes
doors, sliding	portes coulissantes
fitted wardrobe	dressing (m)
key hook	support clé
shelf	étagère (f) or tablette (f)
shelves, set of	rayonnage (m)
shoe rack	support chaussures
tie rack	support cravate
wardrobe	armoire (f)

Wood – le bois

| beading | baguette (f) |
| beech | hêtre (m) |

chestnut	châtaigner (m)
chipboard	aggloméré (m)
hardboard	panneau de fibres dures
hardwood	bois dur or bois exotique
MDF	médium
melamine panel	panneau mélaminé
oak	chêne (m)
pine	sapin (m)
veneer	placage (m)
plywood	contre-plaqué (m)
softwood	bois tendre
solid wood	bois massif
tongue and grooved	à rainure et languette
veneered panel	panneau plaqué
wood panel	panneau (m) de bois

Tools – les outils

allen key	clé allen
bevel square	fausse équerre
brace, of bit and brace	vilebrequin (m)
chisel	ciseau (m)
cutter (Stanley knife)	couteau universel (m)
drill bit	mèche (f)
electric drill	perceuse (f) électrique
electric jig saw	scie sauteuse
electric screwdriver	visseuse (f) électrique
folding rule	mètre (m) pliant
gimlet	vrille (f)
glass cutter	coupe-verre (m)
hammer	marteau (m)
mallet	maillet (m)
metal rule	réglet (m) métallique
nail	clou (m)
pincers	tenaille (f)

plane	rabot (m)
pliers	pince (f)
rasp	râpe (f)
sander	ponceuse (f)
sandpaper	abrasif (m) or papier de verre
saw	scie (f)
saw, circular	scie circulaire
scissors	ciseaux (m) or paire de ciseaux
screw	vis (f)
screwdriver	tournevis (m)
set square	équerre (f) droite
spanner	clé (f)
spanner, adjustable	clé à molette
spanners, set of	jeu de clés
staple gun	forte agrafeuse (f)
T-square	double équerre
tape measure	mètre à ruban
wood glue	colle à bois

06

la plomberie
– plumbing

Almost the same...

The days of 'Napoleon's footsteps' loos are long gone – although there is still one in my local bar in Miramont – so that nowadays plumbing systems look much the same in France and the UK. There are a few visible differences – bathrooms are usually fully tiled, and the washbasins typically have plunger-valves not plugs. The important differences, as you'd expect, are not so visible.

French pipe and fitting sizes are metric – just as UK sizes are metric, but French sizes are properly metric while UK sizes are just conversions of the old Imperial measures. So, in the UK you have 15 mm ($^5/_8$"), 19 mm ($^3/_4$"), 22 mm ($^7/_8$") and the like, while the French sizes are 10 mm, 12 mm, 16 mm, 20 mm, etc. However, you can get converter-connectors that let you join pipes and fittings of different size, so that you can – if you must – use British fittings in a French plumbing system.

The second point you need to note is that French houses have a direct water supply system – there's no cold tank. That'll give you a bit more space in the attic, but the important things in plumbing terms are that your water supply is at mains pressure, and that this is higher than you get in the UK. (If you have ever been flattened against the side in a French shower you'll know this.) In the UK, mains pressure is typically 0.5 bar or less and at most 1 bar. In France, pressure of 3 or 4 bars is normal. If the pressure is so high in your area that it is a problem, you can fit a *détendeur* (regulator) to reduce it to a more reasonable level.

Water is supplied by private companies and is metered, with prices varying and never cheap, compared to the UK. If your house is not on the main drains, your water costs will be lower as there are no sewerage charges.

Check at the mairie

* In some areas, you must fit a *disconnecteur* (isolating valve) to prevent your domestic system flowing back into the mains and polluting the supply. Ask your water company or check at the mairie.

* If you need to install *une fosse septique* (septic tank) you must get your plans approved at the mairie – see page 116.

Les canalisations – pipework

With modern materials and fixings, plumbing can be a job for a *bricoleur* – but even if you are not doing the plumbing yourself, it is helpful to know what the professionals are on about, and what you are paying for.

L'alimentation – supply

The water supply pipework is normally copper, though PER (flexible polyethylene) is increasingly used – and is ideal for the *bricoleur*. On copper pipes, the connections may be *à souder* (soldered) or *à visser* (threaded, i.e. compression).

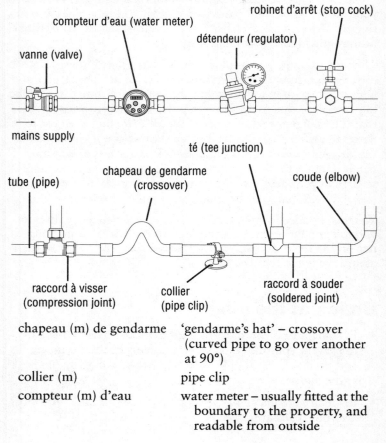

robinet d'arrêt (stop cock)

compteur d'eau (water meter)

détendeur (regulator)

vanne (valve)

mains supply

té (tee junction)

chapeau de gendarme (crossover)

tube (pipe)

coude (elbow)

raccord à visser (compression joint)

collier (pipe clip)

raccord à souder (soldered joint)

chapeau (m) de gendarme	'gendarme's hat' – crossover (curved pipe to go over another at 90°)
collier (m)	pipe clip
compteur (m) d'eau	water meter – usually fitted at the boundary to the property, and readable from outside

coude	corner joint
cuivre recuit	flexible copper piping, sold in rolls
cuivre (m)	copper
cuivre écroui	straight pipes
détendeur (m)	regulator – only needed where high pressure is a problem
disconnecteur (m)	isolating valve
eau de la ville	mains water
manchon (m)	sleeve
PER (polyéthylène réticulé)	polyethylene – flexible piping that can be used instead of copper for hot and cold water supply
plastique	plastic
plomb (m)	lead
PVC	PVC
raccord (m)	joint
raccord coudé	angle joint
raccord à souder	soldered joint
raccord à visser	compression joint
réducteur de pression	pressure reducer
réduction (f)	reducing joint
robinet (m)	tap
robinet d'arrêt	stop cock
robinet de purge	drain cock
té (m)	tee junction
tube (m)	pipe
tuyau (m)	pipe, length of piping
tuyauterie (f)	pipework
vanne (f)	valve, sluice gate

Le réseau d'évacuation – waste water system

There are two systems here: *les gouttières* (guttering) for *les eaux pluviales* (rain water) and the internal system for *les eaux ménagères* ('domestic waters', from sinks and baths) and *les eaux vannes* ('sluice waters', from the toilets).

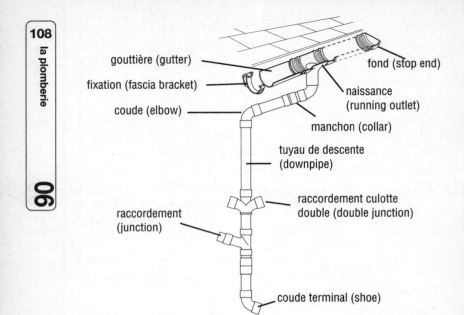

Guttering can be installed by a builder, or by a specialist *zingueur* (zinc worker) – galvanised, i.e. zinc-coated, iron was commonly used for guttering, though most is now PVC.

For the internal systems, carrying *les eaux usées* ('waste water', i.e. all household water from sinks, baths and toilets), you need a *plombier* (plumber).

There may be separate mains drains for rainwater and waste water, and you must connect properly. (In my house, the waste water system had been connected to the rainwater drains, so the first job was to reorganise the plumbing. It's at times like this that you need to make friends with your neighbours!)

amiante-ciment	asbetos cement – once used for drains, this is a health hazard
coude terminal	shoe – the outlet spout at the bottom of the downpipe
dauphin (m)	another name for shoe
eaux (f) pluviales	rain water
eaux ménagères	domestic waters
eaux usées	waste water

eaux vannes	water from toilets
évacuation (f)	waste pipes
fixation (f)	fascia bracket
fond (m)	stop end for gutter
fonte (f)	cast iron
gouttière (f)	gutter
grès (m)	stoneware – commonly used for drains in the past
manchon (m)	collar, coupler
naissance (f)	running outlet, joins gutter to downpipe
raccord (m)	join
raccordement (m)	junction
... culotte double	double junction
tuyau de descente	downpipe
tuyau d'écoulement	overflow
zingué	zinc-coated, galvanised

La salle de bains – the bathroom

If you want a typical French bathroom, you need lots of tiles – ceramic tiles on the floor and right up the walls. Tiles mean lower maintenance and easier cleaning, and cold-to-stand-on after-a-hot-bath is not the same problem in the warmer climate. What you no longer need for your typical French bathroom, is a bidet. Nowadays, most of them take the view that if you have a shower, you do not need a bidet, and a shower makes better use of the space.

As an alternative to an ordinary shower, you can have a hydromassage – one with horizontal jets that can pound you from the side. You can get self-contained *cabines hydromassantes* (hydro-massage cubicles), or fit a *colonne de douche hydromassante* (hydromassage column) instead of an ordinary shower head – just make sure that your cubicle is watertight!

Une colonne de douche hydromassante

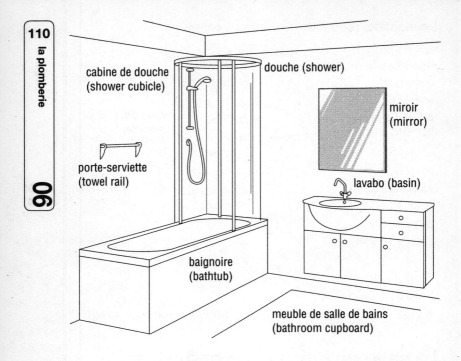

cabine de douche
(shower cubicle)

douche (shower)

miroir
(mirror)

porte-serviette
(towel rail)

lavabo (basin)

baignoire
(bathtub)

meuble de salle de bains
(bathroom cupboard)

Mixer taps

Mixer taps are the norm for basins, baths and showers. There are two sorts of mixer taps: a mélangeur has separate hot and cold controls; a mitigeur has a single lever which controls the volume and temperature. A mitigeur is a better choice for a shower as you can turn the water on and off without having to find the right hot-cold balance every time.

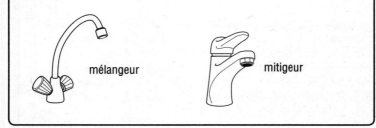

mélangeur

mitigeur

Le lavabo (the basin)

Most basins have combination mixer taps and lever-operated plughole covers.

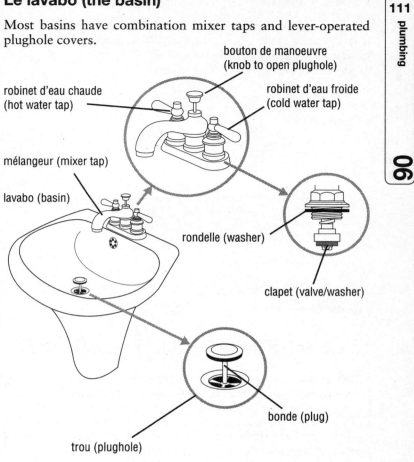

bouton de manoeuvre
(knob to open plughole)

robinet d'eau chaude
(hot water tap)

robinet d'eau froide
(cold water tap)

mélangeur (mixer tap)

lavabo (basin)

rondelle (washer)

clapet (valve/washer)

bonde (plug)

trou (plughole)

La vasque – washbowl

Instead of a *lavabo* (basin), you could have a *vasque* (bowl). This can be fitted *à poser* – freestanding on top of a vanity unit, or *à encastrer* – embedded into the unit like a basin.

Le WC – the loo

It's one of those ironies of language that what we call the 'loo', from *l'eau* (the water), the French call WC (pronounced 'vay-say'), from water closet. The technology is the same, though they seem to prefer the button flush mechanisms.

réservoir (cistern)

porte-papier
(loo roll holder)

balai (toilet brush)

abattant (seat and lid)

porte-balai
(brush holder)

cuvette (lavatory bowl)

Lexicon: la salle de bains – bathroom

abattant (m)	WC seat lid
adoucisseur (m)	water softening system
anneau (m)	(towel) ring
armoire (f) à pharmacie	medicine cabinet
armoire (f) de toilette	bathroom cabinet
bac	shower tray
baignoire (f)	bathtub
bain (m)	bath
balai (m)	toilet brush
bidet (m)	bidet
bonde (f)	plug
bouton (m) de manoeuvre	knob
cabine de douche	shower cubicle
cabinet (m)	lavatory

caillebotis (m)	duckboard/grating for stepping on after having a bath or shower
chasse d'eau (f)	WC cistern
chauffe-eau (m)	water heater
cuvette de w.c. (f)	toilet pan
douche (f)	shower
éléments sanitaires	sanitary ware
gant de toilette (m)	facecloth
hydromassage (m)	hydromassage cabinet/system
hydromassant	hydromassaging
installations (f)	fittings
lavabo (m)	basin
lave-mains (m)	handbasin
mécanisme de chasse	flushing mechanism
mélangeur (m)	mixer tap with separate controls
meuble à carreler	tiled bathroom cupboard
meuble WC	cupboard behind/over WC
miroir (m)	mirror
mitigeur (m)	mixer tap with combined volume/ temperature control
panier en rotin	rattan laundry basket
parois (m) de douche	shower screen
pèse-personne (m)	scales
plan (m) de verre	glass washbasin surround
porte-balai (m)	brush and holder
porte-gant (m)	facecloth hook
porte-papier (m)	loo roll holder
porte-peignoirs (m)	hook for peignoir (dressing gown)
porte-savon (m)	soap dish
porte-serviettes (m)	towel rail
porte-verre (m)	toothmug holder
poubelle (f)	rubbish bin
poubelle (f) à pédale	pedal bin
réservoir (m)	cistern

robinet (m)…	tap
… d'eau chaude	hot water tap
… d'eau froide	cold water tap
rondelle (f)	washer
sèche-serviette (m)	heated towel rail
siphon (m)	U-bend
siphon à bague	threaded 'ring' trap
siphon bouteille	bottle trap
siphon en forme de S	S-bend
tablette (f)	small shelf
valet (m) de douche	shower tidy
vasque (f)	washbasin bowl – freestanding (à poser) or embedded (à encastrer)
vidange (f)	waste pipes, from basin or bath
WC avec broyeur	loo with grinder, allows WC to feed into ordinary waste pipes

La cuisine – kitchen

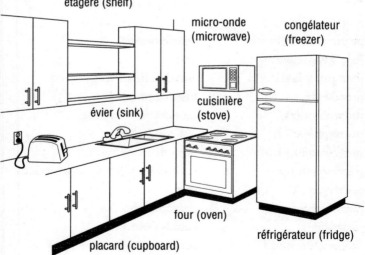

étagère (shelf)
micro-onde (microwave)
congélateur (freezer)
cuisinière (stove)
évier (sink)
four (oven)
réfrigérateur (fridge)
placard (cupboard)

I suspect that the main difference between the average kitchens in France and the UK is in the quality of the food – which is one of the reasons why we love France, isn't it? The appliances and fittings are much the same.

L'évier – the sink

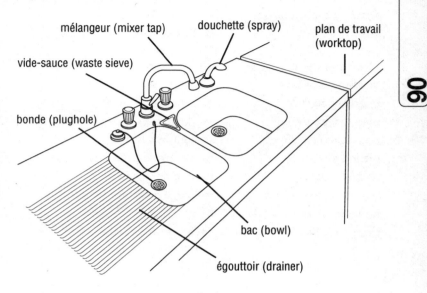

mélangeur (mixer tap)

douchette (spray)

plan de travail (worktop)

vide-sauce (waste sieve)

bonde (plughole)

bac (bowl)

égouttoir (drainer)

aspiration (f)	ventilation
bac (m)	bowl
bac (m) à laver	laundry sink (deep)
bonde (f)	plug or plughole
buanderie (f)	laundry, wash house
caoutchouc	rubber
congélateur (m)	freezer
couvre-joint (m)	sealing strip (tiles/worksurfaces)
cuisinière (f)	stove
cuisson (f)	cooking
cuve (f)	stand-alone sink
débouchoir (m)	plunger
douchette (f)	spray

égouttoir (m)	drainer
évier (m)	kitchen sink
façade (f)	front (doors and drawer)
four (m)	oven
foyer (m)	burner in hob
hotte (f) aspirante	cooker hood
inox	stainless steel, from *inoxydable* meaning rustproof
lave-vaisselle (m)	dishwasher
machine (f) à laver	washing machine
micro-onde (m)	microwave
plan (m) de travail	work surface
poubelle (f) à clapet	swing bin
réfrigérateur (m)	fridge, often called *un frigo*
sèche-linge (m)	tumble dryer
stratifiés postformés	roll edge laminate (postformed)
table de cuisson (f)	hob
timbre d'office	deep ceramic (Belfast) sink – *une timbre* is a drinking trough for animals (*une timbre* is also a stamp!)
trop-plein (m)	overflow
ventouse (f)	sink plunger
vide-sauce (m)	waste sieve

La fosse septique – the septic tank

If your house is not *tout à l'égout* (on mains drains), then you are going to need *une fosse septique* (septic tank) – or a *micro-station d'épuration* (purification micro-station). If you have an old *fosse*, you may need a new one – or a *micro-station*. The French government is working to improve the (already good) water quality and to reduce pollution of groundwater.

But first, what is a *fosse septique*? They vary, but essentially a *fosse* is a system of chambers, dug in the ground near the house.

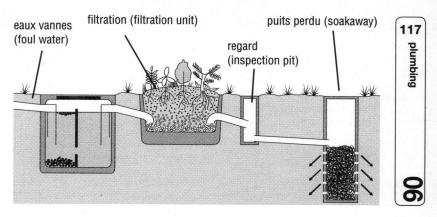

eaux vannes (foul water)

filtration (filtration unit)

regard (inspection pit)

puits perdu (soakaway)

The first chamber is a watertight tank into which the toilet and house drains empty foul water. Solid matter is broken down by bacteriological action – a process which takes around a week. Not all solid matter breaks down, which is why you must call out the *vidangeur* (septic tank emptier) every three or four years.

The second chamber is the filtration unit, typically a bed of sand. This may be closed, or capped with earth with grass or small plants growing above. (Trees and bushes must be kept away from *fosses* because their roots can damage the structures.)

The final chamber is the *puits perdu* (soakaway) – a porous pit filled with rubble or gravel. The filtration unit and soakaway can be combined into one, or if the filtered water can be released into a stream, the soakaway may not be necessary.

Are the mains coming?

Before you go any further with your plans for a new fosse, check at the mairie. The French are trying to put as many houses as possible onto mains drains – it's the best way to assure water quality – so there is a programme of drain construction in hand that is reaching ever deeper into the countryside.

Ask at the mairie about the plans for your area.

A *fosse* system takes some space – a minimum of 150m² free from trees and shrubs. If there isn't that much space available in the garden, then there is an alternative – *le micro-station d'épuration*

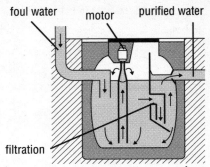

foul water   motor   purified water

filtration

(purification microstation). This is a motorised system that circulates and aerates the water, to produce a faster breakdown of solids. As it is faster, less storage volume is required, and as it has its own filtration system, the whole structure is far more compact.

The *fosse* system may also have a separate grease trap, where grease, oil and other floating nasties will collect at the top, and must be removed periodically. The grease trap may be integral to the *fosse* – but the floating gunge still needs removal.

A new *fosse* must meet stringent standards on water quality, and cannot be constructed without a *permis d'assainissement* (permit to allow water to drain). These are issued by the mairie, which is where you must start. Go to the *bureau d'études* (research department), who will advise on how large a *fosse* you need and where – and if – it can be located on your land.

The simplest solution is probably to put the whole business in the hands of a *fosse* building firm. They will know the ropes, and you'll have to hire them anyway unless you want to dig those holes yourself and manhandle the tanks into place! The cost of getting them to deal with the bureaucracy will be small in comparison to the cost of the installation. Depending upon the size of the *fosse*, the nature of the land and other factors, this should be in the region of €5,000 to €10,000.

The fosse way

Fosses septiques and micro-stations are organic systems that are designed for dealing with organic matter. They cannot cope with cigarette ends, tampons, préservatifs (condoms) and other indigestible objects that people routinely flush down the toilet. Bleach, paint, white spirit, and other harsh chemicals cannot be flushed either, as these will kill the bacteria that make the fosse work. Ordinary soap is not a problem, and there are washing powders and cleaners that are safe for use with fosse systems. Look after your fosse and your fosse will look after you!

bureau d'études	research department
épuration (f)	purification
eaux d'égout	sewage
eaux vannes	foul water
filtration (f)	filtration unit
fosse (f) septique	septic tank
permis d'assainissement	permit to drain water from land
puits (m) filtrant	soakaway – literally filtering well
regard (m)	inspection pit
tuyau d'égout (m)	soil pipe
vidangeur (m)	septic tank emptier

Les outils – tools

clé anglaise
(adjustable spanner)

clé à griffe
(pipewrench)

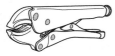

pince étau (mole grip)

pince coupante (cutters)

coup tube (pipe cutter)

lampe à souder (soldering lamp)

chalumeau (m)	blow lamp
clé (f)	spanner
clé anglaise	adjustable spanner
clé à griffe	pipewrench
coupe tube (m)	pipe cutter

lampe (f) à souder	soldering lamp
pince (f) étau	mole grip, wrench
pince coupante	cutters (for PVC pipes)
sacoche (f) de plombier	plumber's bag, usually soft leather
scie à métaux	hacksaw
ventouse (f)	plunger

The essential plumbing term

When you need this, you won't have time to learn it, so learn it now.

'Au secours, il y a une fuite! ' (Help, there's a leak.)

English–French quick reference

Pipework – les canalisations

asbetos cement	amiante-ciment
cast iron	fonte (f)
copper	cuivre (m)
downpipe	tuyau de descent
drain cock	robinet de purge
elbow joint	coude
galvanised	zingué
gutter	gouttière (f)
joint...	raccord (m) ...
... soldered	... à souder
... compression	... à visser
junction	raccordement (m)
lead	plomb (m)
mains water	eau de la ville
pipe	tube (m), tuyau (m)
pipe clip	collier (m)

plastic	plastique
regulator	détendeur (m)
stoneware	grès (m)
stop cock	robinet d'arrêt
valve	vanne (f)
waste water system	réseau d'évacuation
water meter	compteur (m) d'eau

Bathroom – la salle de bains

basin	lavabo (m), vasque (m)
bathtub	baignoire (f)
glass washbasin surround	plan (m) de verre
hydromassage cabinet	hydromassage (m)
laundry basket	panier (m)
lavatory	cabinet (m)
medicine cabinet	armoire (f) à pharmacie
mirror	miroir (m)
mixer tap	mélangeur (m), mitigeur (m)
plug	bonde (f)
rubbish bin	poubelle (f)
sanitary ware	éléments sanitaires
scales	pèse-personne (m)
shower	douche (f)
shower cubicle	cabine de douche
shower tray	bac (m)
soap dish	porte-savon (m)
tap	robinet (m)
toilet brush	balai (m)
toilet pan	cuvette de w.c. (f)
toilet roll holder	porte-papier (m)
toothmug holder	porte-verre (m)
towel rail	porte-serviettes (m)
towel rail, heated	sèche-serviette (m)
towel ring	anneau (m)

U-bend	siphon (m)
washer	rondelle (f)
waste pipes	vidange (f)
WC cistern	chasse d'eau (f)
WC seat lid	abattant (m)

Kitchen – la cuisine

bowl	bac (m)
burner in hob	foyer (m)
cooker hood	hotte (f) aspirante
dishwasher	lave-vaisselle (m)
drainer	égouttoir (m)
freezer	congélateur (m)
fridge	réfrigérateur
hob	table de cuisson (f)
kitchen sink	évier (m)
microwave	micro-onde (m)
oven	four (m)
overflow	trop-plein (m)
plug(hole)	bonde (f)
rubber	caoutchouc
sink plunger	débouchoir (m), ventouse (f)
spray	douchette (f)
stainless steel	inox
stove	cuisinière (f)
swing bin	poubelle (f) à clapet
tumble dryer	sèche-linge (m)
washing machine	machine (m) à laver
work surface	plan (m) de travail
waste sieve	vide-sauce (m)

Septic tank – la fosse septique

| filtration unit | filtration (f) |
| foul water | eaux vannes |

inspection pit	regard (m)
permit to drain water	permis d'assainissement
purification	épuration (f)
septic tank	fosse (f) septique
septic tank emptier	vidangeur (m)
sewage	eaux d'égout
soakaway	puits (m) perdu
soil pipe	tuyau d'égout (m)

Tools – les outils

adjustable spanner	clé anglaise
blow lamp	chalumeau (m)
cutters (for PVC pipes)	pince coupante
hacksaw	scie à métaux
mole grip	pince (f) étau
pipe cutter	coupe tube (m)
pipewrench	clé à griffe
plumber's bag	sacoche (f) de plombier
soldering lamp	lampe (f) à souder
spanner	clé (f)

07

le chauffage et l'électricité – heating and electricity

Almost the same...

Heating and lighting appliances and usages are actually very similar in the UK and France. If many of us feel that things are different, it is probably because we are comparing UK town life with French rural life.

With electricity, the most obvious difference is that in France there are several levels of power supply. Like us they have a plethora of tariffs, but all theirs are offered by one firm instead of a mass of competing firms. Power supplies are less reliable than in the UK, especially in rural areas, mainly because they seem to be more susceptible to bad weather. Thunderstorms are a common cause of disruption – and of damage. You must turn off TVs and computers during storms, and disconnect aerials. You should also install surge protection and UPS (uninterruptible power supply) if you use a computer for work.

With gas, there is a more widespread use of bottled or tank gas, simply because piped gas does not extend much beyond towns.

Wood is used more as a fuel. Supplies are plentiful, prices are competitive and rural houses generally have the space to store large stocks.

Le chauffage – heating

The first question is, which fuel(s) will you use? You have quite a choice:

- *Bois* (wood) is very popular – around 30% of all French houses have a wood-burning fire or *poêle* (stove). It is bought by the *stère* (cubic metre), and must be stored for at least a few months before it is needed – green wood produces a lot of tar which condenses in the chimney and creates problems.

- *Charbon* (coal) can be used instead of or with wood. If you want to run central heating from a solid fuel stove, coal is more efficient and cheaper, but wood is cleaner to handle.

- *Fuel domestique* (oil) also called *fioul* and *mazout*, is widely used for running central heating systems in rural areas. The installation of a *un réservoir fixe* (tank) is not cheap, and the cost of fuel varies with the price of crude oil.

- *Gaz* (gas) comes in three varieties: *gaz de ville* (town gas), supplied by GDF – Gaz de France – is a convenient option, where it is available. Propane can be stored, like fuel oil, in a large *réservoir fixe* (tank) either *aérien* (above ground) or *enterré* (underground). Butane, and propane, can also be bought *en bouteille* (in bottles).

- *Electricité* (electricity) is relatively cheaper in France than in the UK, and is well worth considering as a heating fuel. Electric heating systems are also simpler to install than gas-fired radiator systems. Look at EDF's tariffs with cheaper off-peak rates if you are thinking about this.

What is right for you will depend upon the nature of your house and the way that you intend to use it.

- Is there *une cheminée* (fireplace) or can one be installed?

- If the house is in an urban area, are there restrictions on solid fuel fires?

- How much storage space do you have for solid fuel, or for oil/gas tanks?

- If the house is not connected to mains gas, can it be connected, and at what cost?

- Will the house be used mainly in the summer, or at times throughout the year, or will it be your permanent home? If you only need the occasional heating on chilly evenings, the cost and efficiency of the fuel is a minor consideration.

Le chauffage central – central heating

Chauffage à eau (heating by water) generally works by means of *radiateurs*, though *plancher chauffant* (underfloor heating) is a possible alternative.

A modern French system is well regulated. A *sonde extérieure* (external sensor) picks up the outside temperature and adjusts the temperature of the circulating water appropriately. Within the house, a *thermostat d'ambiance* (area thermostat) will control the heat in a zone or room, while a *robinet thermostatique* (radiator thermostat) can control individual radiators.

The *chaudière* (boiler) can be *murale* (wall-mounted) or *au sol* (free-standing).

Le chauffage central – central heating

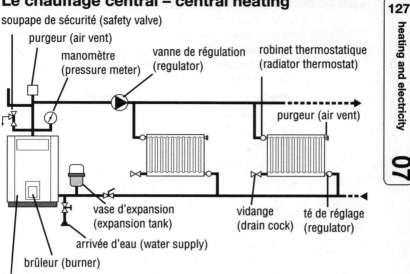

soupape de sécurité (safety valve)

purgeur (air vent)

manomètre (pressure meter)

vanne de régulation (regulator)

robinet thermostatique (radiator thermostat)

purgeur (air vent)

vase d'expansion (expansion tank)

vidange (drain cock)

té de réglage (regulator)

arrivée d'eau (water supply)

brûleur (burner)

chaudière (boiler)

La cheminée – the fireplace

An open fire is always attractive, though lumping in the logs or buckets of coal and clearing out the ash can become a chore if you have to do it regularly.

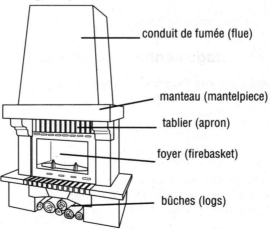

conduit de fumée (flue)

manteau (mantelpiece)

tablier (apron)

foyer (firebasket)

bûches (logs)

Cheminées tend to be rather grand, built from thick stone and heavy beams.

Les appareils de chauffage – heating equipment

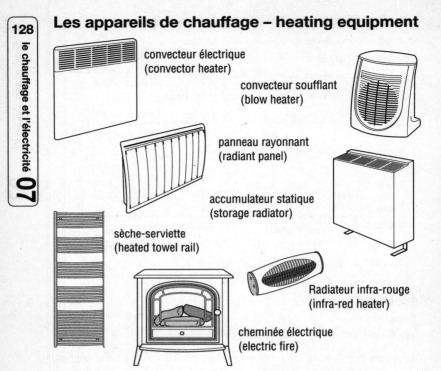

convecteur électrique
(convector heater)

convecteur soufflant
(blow heater)

panneau rayonnant
(radiant panel)

accumulateur statique
(storage radiator)

sèche-serviette
(heated towel rail)

Radiateur infra-rouge
(infra-red heater)

cheminée électrique
(electric fire)

Lexicon: le chauffage – heating

accumulateur statique	storage radiator – very economic if you use an off-peak tariff
arrivée d'eau (f)	incoming water supply
bois (m)	wood
boisseau (m)	chimney-flue tile
bouteille (f)	bottle, e.g. for butane
brûleur (m)	burner in boiler
bûche (f)	log
cendrier (m)	cinder tray
charbon (m)	coal
chaudière au sol	free-standing boiler
chaudière (f) murale	wall-mounted boiler
chauffage à air pulsé	hot-air heating

chauffage à eau	heating by water
cheminée électrique	electric fire
conduit de fumée	flue
contre-coeur (m)	fire-back
convecteur (m) électrique	convector heater
convecteur soufflant	blow heater
électricité (f)	electricity
foyer (m)	firebasket
fuel domestique	heating oil
gaz de ville	town gas
manomètre (m)	pressure meter
manteau (m)	mantelpiece
mazout	heating oil
panneau rayonnant	radiant panel
poêle (m)	stove
poêle à bois	wood burning stove
poêle cheminée	wood burning stove with flue
programmateur centralisé	heating controls
propane liquide	LPG – liquid propane gas
purgeur (m)	air vent
radiateur (m) à fluide	oil-filled radiator
radiateur infra-rouge	infra-red heater
ramoneur (m)	chimneysweep
réservoir fixe (m)	tank for oil or propane
robinet thermostatique	radiator thermostat
sèche-serviette (m)	heated towel rail
sonde (f)	sensor
soupape de sécurité (f)	safety valve
tablier (m)	apron – lining above and/or below hearth in a fireplace
té (m) de réglage	regulator/stop cock on radiator
thermostat d'ambiance	area thermostat
vase d'expansion (m)	expansion tank
vidange (f)	drain cock

Heating and lightning

If you have a fuel-oil or propane tank it must be earthed. Some friends, enjoying a dramatic thunderstorm one night, watched in horror as lightning struck their oil tank. It glowed bright blue, but fortunately nothing else happened! They had a lightning conductor fitted the next day.

Their luck didn't hold though that night – another strike fried their TV, video, satellite box and most of the telephone wiring and sockets in the house.

L'alimentation d'électricité – the electricity supply

If you are having your electrical supply installed or reinstalled, you will have to decide which *puissance* (power supply level) will best suit. There are nine possible power ratings, ranging upwards from 3kVA. In practice, most houses will need a supply in the range 6kVA to 15kVA.

* 6kVA will be enough to power simultaneously the lights, three or four small appliances, e.g. TV, fridge, hoover, and a single more power-hungry appliance such as a washing machine or an electric cooker.

* 9kVA will also handle a second large appliance.

* 12kVA is the minimum if electricity is also used for heating, and would be sufficient for a house of up to 100m².

* 15kVA will handle the power and heating for a larger house.

You would only need to go to 18kVA if you have a very large, all-electric house, or you use heavy machinery in your work.

Rewiring tends to be more expensive than in the UK, though as with all work on a house, using a registered tradesman means that you have a guarantee of quality. You must have a registered electrician to connect you to the mains – EDF insist on this.

The incoming electricity supply, up to the *compteur* (meter) and the *disjoncteur de branchement* (mains switch), is the responsibility of EDF.

Monophasé and triphasé

In France, there are two distinct types of electricity supply. Monophasé is the same as our 230 volt domestic supply. Triphasé provides both 230 and 400 volts supply and is mainly designed for industrial use. (Triphasé is delivered down three live wires, instead of one, which is why the voltage can be higher.) It's what's usually supplied to farms to power their machinery, but if your house is in the countryside, it may be what is supplied to you. If you have a 18kVA or higher puissance, it will probably be supplied as triphasé. In practice, having triphasé doesn't create any problems, as normal domestic equipment can be run off it simply by selecting the 230 volt supply.

Les fusibles et les disjoncteurs – fuses and circuit breakers

A modern *boîte à fusibles* (fuse box) doesn't have *fusibles* (fuses), but instead has a *disjoncteur* (cut-out) or *coupe circuit* (circuit breaker) on each branch.

The best *disjoncteurs* are the differential variety, which give greater protection against electric shocks. They have a normal magnothermal cut-out which is triggered by a surge in the voltage or a short circuit, and a cut-out which responds to a change in the differential between the live and the neutral wires.

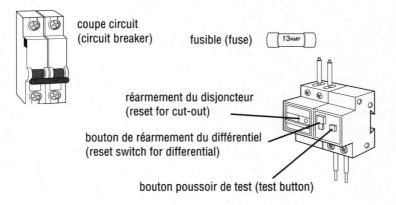

coupe circuit
(circuit breaker)

fusible (fuse)   13AMP

réarmement du disjoncteur
(reset for cut-out)

bouton de réarmement du différentiel
(reset switch for differential)

bouton poussoir de test (test button)

Sockets

The French use round-pin *prises de courant* (electric sockets). There are two types: *2 pôles* (2-pin) for lamps and *2 pôles + terre* (2-pin + earth) for everything else. (The earth connects through a pin on the socket and a hole on the plug.)

prise 2 pôles + terre (2-pin + earth)

UK appliances will work perfectly well in France – as long as you have plug adaptors – but it's usually best to buy French. You don't have the plug problem and it's easier to take it back if it doesn't work.

Note the same word, *prise*, is used for both 'plug' and 'socket'. If you need to be specific, ask for *une prise mâle* for a plug or *une prise femelle* for a socket.

Phone connections

Telephone plugs and sockets are also different shapes to those in the UK, so buy your phones in France as well.

L'électricité – electricity

alimentation (f) électrique	electrical supply
bloc multi-prise	multi-socket
câble (m)	cable
compteur (m)	meter
conjoncteur (m)	mains supply point
courant alternatif	AC
courant (m) électrique	electric current
court-circuit (m)	short circuit
disjoncteur (m)…	circuit breaker
… de branchement (m)	mains switch
… différentiel	differential cut-out
faire sauter les plombs	blow the fuses

fiche (f)	plug (or socket) – another term, and the same dual use
fil fusible	wire fuse
fusible (m)	fuse
fusible à cartouche	cartridge fuse
neutre (m)	neutral wire
phase (f)	live wire
prise du terre	plug with earth pin
prise 2 pôles + terre	2-pin + earth socket
puissance (f)	power level
tension (m) de courant	voltage
terre (f)	earth (wire)

Les chauffe-eau – water heaters

There are two main types of *chauffe-eau* – the on-demand boilers, either gas or electric, which are all but identical to those in the UK, and the electric *ballons d'eau chaude* (hot-water tank), which work like a tank with an immersion heater, but look somewhat different.

These slim cylinders are wall-mounted or free-standing, depending on size, and range from 50 litres (sufficient for a kitchen sink) to 300 litres (bath water for a family). The heating element is normally of between 1kW and 2kW, which makes for relatively slow heating – typically 4 or 5 hours for a tankful – but you don't have to increase your power supply level to run one.

chauffe-eau électrique (electric water heater)

Les appareils électriques – electrical appliances

The electrical appliances are all but the same in France and the UK – hardly surprising as they are largely from the same firms.

You may have to hunt around a little to find a *bouilloire* (kettle), as they are not regularly used by the French. Well, if you don't drink tea and you have a *cafetière* and a *tire-bouchon* (cork screw), what's the point of a kettle?

cuisinière (cooker)

table de cuisson (hob)

four (oven)

lave-vaisselle (dishwasher)

lave-linge (washing machine)

cave à vin (wine store)

robot (food processor)

grille-pain (toaster)

caméscope (video camera)

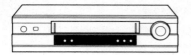
magnétoscope (video recorder/player)

téléviseur (TV)

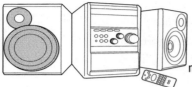
microchaîne (hi-fi mini-stack)

Les appareils électriques – electrical appliances

ampli (m)	amplifier
armoire (f) à vin	(electric) wine cabinet, controlled temperature and humidity
aspirateur (m)	vacuum cleaner
baguette (f)	cable cover
ballon (m)	(hot water) tank
boîte à fusibles (f)	fuse box
bouilloire (f)	kettle
cafetière (f)	coffee maker
caméscope (m)	video camera
cave (f) à vin	(electric) wine cabinet
chauffe-eau (m)	water heater
congélateur (m)	freezer
cuisinière (f)	cooker
écran plat	flat screen
enceinter (f)	speaker
fer à repasser (m)	iron
four à poser	free-standing oven
four encastrable	built-in oven
réfrigérateur (m)	fridge
grille-pain (m)	toaster
lave-linge (m)	washing machine

lave-vaisselle (m)	dishwasher
lecteur DVD (m)	DVD player
magnétoscope (m)	video recorder/player
microchaîne (f)	mini hi-fi stack system
micro-ordinateur (m)	micro computer, PC
mixeur (m)	hand-held mixer
numérique	digital
ordinateur (m)	computer
parabole (f)	TV satellite dish
platine (f) cassette	tape deck
platine laser	CD player
réfrigérateur (m)	refrigerator
répondeur (m)	answering machine
robot (m)	food processor, also used to refer to other clever machinery – ask for a *robot de cuisine* to make sure
sèche-linge (m)	tumble dryer
table de cuisson	hob
téléphone (m)	telephone
téléviseur 4/3ème	standard TV – 4/3 is the aspect (width to height) ratio
téléviseur 16/9ème	widescreen TV
trépied (m)	tripod stand for *chauffe-eau*
tuner (m)	radio tuner

French TV

French TV is unique in using the SECAM technology – the rest of Europe follows the PAL standard. A UK TV set will not be able to receive French broadcasts – though it will be fine for Sky. French TV sets can handle both technologies. Do note that French TV retailers are obliged to pass your name and address on to the licensing authorities. You still need to pay your licence fee, even if you only watch Sky and British videos. The fee is collected along with the local tax. If you do not have a TV, you can claim exemption.

Les luminaires – light fittings

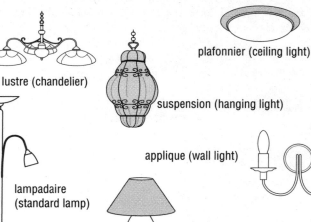

plafonnier (ceiling light)

lustre (chandelier)

suspension (hanging light)

applique (wall light)

lampadaire
(standard lamp)

lampe (lamp)

ampoule (f)	light bulb
applique (f)	wall light
douille (f)	light socket
éclairage (m)	lighting
halogène	halogen
interrupteur (m)	light switch
interrupteur (m) va et vient	two-way switch
lampadaire (m)	lampstand
lampe (f)	lamp
lampe de lecteur	reading lamp
lampe éco énergie	energy-saving lightbulb
lumière (f)	light
lustre (m)	multi-bulb centre light, chandelier
lustre à 4 lumières	4-bulb centre light
plafonnier (m)	ceiling light
spot (m)	spotlight
suspension (f)	hanging light
tube fluorescent (m)	fluorescent light

Les outils – tools

There are few special tools for electrical work – although they make electrician's versions of hammers, chisels, knifes and other tools.

détecteur de cable (cable detector)

tournevis testeur
(screwdriver/current tester)

pinces à dénuder isolées
(wire cutters/strippers)

détecteur de cable	cable detector
pinces à dénuder isolées	wire cutters/strippers
pince ampèrémétrique	meter
ruban adhésif isolant	insulating tape
tournevis testeur	screwdriver/voltage tester, also called *tournevis détecteur de tension*

L'énergie solaire – solar energy

In case you hadn't noticed, France is a sunnier country than the UK, and this makes solar energy more viable. Les capteurs solaires thermiques (solar panels) can provide 50% to 80% of the water heating needs, so an installation could more than pay for itself over time if you are there a significant part of the year. If the French house is your main residence, you can also get a government grant towards the cost.

Les modules photovoltaïques (solar cells) for electricity generation may also be worth investigating.

As these may change the appearance of your house, you will need to get planning permission – ask at the mairie.

English–French quick reference

Heating – le chauffage

air vent	purgeur (m)
blow heater	convecteur soufflant
boiler	chaudière (f)
central heating controls	programmateur centralisé
chimneysweep	ramoneur (m)
cinder tray	cendrier (m)
coal	charbon (m)
convector heater	convecteur (m) électrique
electric fire	cheminée (f) électrique
firebasket	foyer (m)
flue	conduit de fumée
heated towel rail	sèche-serviette (m)
heating oil	fuel domestique, mazout
infra-red heater	radiateur (m) infra-rouge
log	bûche (f)
mantelpiece	manteau (m)
radiator	radiateur (m)
radiator thermostat	robinet thermostatique
sensor	sonde (f)
storage radiator	accumulateur (m) statique
stove	poêle (m)
town gas	gaz de ville
wood	bois (m)

Electricity – l'électricité

AC	courant alternatif
blow the fuses	faire sauter les plombs
circuit breaker	disjoncteur (m)
earth (wire)	terre (f)
electric current	courant (m) électrique

electrical supply	alimentation (f) électrique
fuse	fusible (m)
fuse, cartridge	fusible à cartouche
fuse wire	fil fusible
live wire	phase (f)
mains supply point	conjoncteur (m)
mains switch	disjoncteur de branchement
meter	compteur (m)
neutral wire	neutre (m)
plug/socket	prise (f)
power level	puissance (f)
short circuit	court-circuit (m)
voltage	tension (f) du courant

Electrical appliances – les appareils électriques

amplifier	ampli (m)
answering machine	répondeur (m)
cable cover	baguette (f)
CD player	platine laser
coffee maker	cafetière (f)
computer	ordinateur (m)
cooker	cuisinière (f)
digital	numérique
dishwasher	lave-vaisselle (m)
DVD player	lecteur DVD (m)
flat screen	écran plat
food processor	robot (m)
freezer	congélateur (m)
fridge	réfrigérateur (m)
fuse box	boîte à fusibles (f)
hand-held mixer	mixeur (m)
hob	table de cuisson
iron	fer à repasser (m)
kettle	bouilloire (f)

mini hi-fi stack system	microchaîne (f)
oven	four
radio tuner	tuner (m)
speaker	enceinte (f)
tape deck	platine (f) cassette
telephone	téléphone (m)
toaster	grille-pain (m)
tumble dryer	sèche-linge (m)
TV, standard	téléviseur 4/3ème
TV, widescreen	téléviseur 16/9ème
vacuum cleaner	aspirateur (m)
video camera	caméscope (m)
video recorder/player	magnétoscope (m)
washing machine	lave-linge (m)
wine cabinet	armoire à vin, cave (f) à vin

Light fittings – les luminaires

ceiling light	plafonnier (m)
chandelier	lustre (m)
energy-saving lightbulb	lamp (f) éco énergie
fluorescent light	tube fluorescent (m)
hanging light	suspension (f)
lamp	lampe (f)
lampstand	lampadaire (m)
light	lumière (f)
light bulb	ampoule (f)
light socket	douille (f)
light switch	interrupteur (m)
lighting	éclairage (m)
reading lamp	lampe de lecteur, liseuse (f)
spot light	spot (m)
two-way switch	interrupteur (m) va et vient
wall light	applique (f)

08

la décoration
– decorating

Almost the same...

French style in decoration and furnishings is – overall – a little different to ours. Obviously, you will find a huge variety and range of styles in people's houses in France, just as you will in the UK, and these ranges very largely overlap. (You can't escape IKEA.) But, walk round the popular decoration and furnishing stores in both countries and you will see what I mean. French furniture and furnishings tend to be a little more ornate, and the wallpaper tends to have heavier patterns, though the colours of their paints – especially the emulsion ranges – seem to be more muted. Having said that, some French houses can be quite spartan in the simplicity. Every room in my house had plain painted walls and natural woodwork – unfortunately, they'd used the same duck egg blue throughout!

I am not saying that you should try for a French look because it is a French house. It's your house, so it should have your look. What I am saying is this. Don't expect to find the same colours and patterns at Mr Brico that you would in B&Q, and don't whinge about it. *Vive la différence!*

Check at the mairie

- If you are thinking about painting the outside walls or the shutters, look around at your neighbours' houses first. If they all use the same colours, or a very restricted range of colours, the *commune* may have rules on external decorations. Ask at the *mairie* before you paint anything. It will only take 10 minutes and it could save you days of repainting.

- Likewise, if you live within sight of a historic building, check at the *mairie* before you paint the outside.

La peinture – paint

I've heard people be very rude about cheap French paint. And it is true. Cheap French paint is just as bad as cheap British paint. The only time I ever use it is for the first coat or two on fresh plaster, which will soak any paint up like blotting paper. Good French paint is just as good as in the UK – it should be as it's from the same manufacturers – though the colour ranges are a little different (and there is far less choice in France).

If a paint is *glycéro*, it is oil-based. (And *glycéro* is short for *glycérophtalique* in case you are interested.) Other types of paints are *acrylique* (acrylic, of course), *microporeuse* (micro-porous for external woodwork) and special paints for *sol* (floors), *plafond* (ceilings), *métal* (metal), *volets* (shutters) and *façades* (exterior walls).

L'aspect (the finish) can be *mat* (matt), *satiné* (satin), *velouté* (silk) or *brillant* (gloss).

If you want a non-drip paint, ask for *anti-goutte*, and for one-coat paint, ask for *monocouche*. (And good luck to you – one coat never does it for me, with either French or British paints!)

acrylique	acrylic
aérosol	aerosol
anti-goutte	non-drip
apprêt (m)	undercoat
aspect (m)	finish, e.g. *l'aspect mat*
brillant	gloss
glycéro	*glycérophtalique*, oil-based
lasure (f)	wood stain
mat	matt
microporeuse	microporous
monocouche	one-coat
peinture (f)	paint
peinture d'impression	primer
peinture façade	masonry paint
satiné	satin finish
sous-couche (f)	undercoat
teinture (f)	wood stain
térébenthine (f)	turpentine
touche (f) d'essais	test pot
velouté	silk
vernis (m)	varnish
white spirit	white spirit – same in French

Les outils – tools

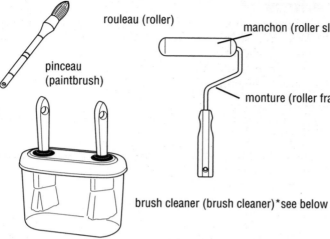

rouleau (roller)

manchon (roller sleeve)

pinceau
(paintbrush)

monture (roller frame)

brush cleaner (brush cleaner)*see below

bac à peinture	paint tray
bâche (f)	dust sheet
brosse (f)	brush
brush cleaner	brush cleaner – don't ask me why this is the same in French, but note that it refers to the cleaning bath, not the solution
chiffon (m)	paper towel, literally 'rag'
manchon (m)	roller sleeve
monture (f)	roller frame
perche télescopique	telescopic handle (for roller)
pinceau (m)	paintbrush, round or flat
rouleau (m)	roller
ruban (m) de masquage	masking tape

Round brushes

Round paint brushes are much more popular in France than they are in the UK. You have to adjust your technique a little, but you can get a good edge with these.

Les revêtements muraux – wall coverings

Researching this book made me look a little further round the *bricolages* (DIY stores) that I would otherwise have done, which is how I found *toile de verre* (glass fibre wall covering). This is a tough alternative to lining paper that can give a smooth finish to cracked walls and ceilings. (Only minor cracks – it won't hold rotting plaster together.)

colle (f)	paste
colle murale (f)	wallpaper paste
dalle (f) de liège	cork tile
mini-maille	fine mesh
papier peint (m)	wallpaper
papier peint à peindre	lining paper
papier peint vinyl	vinyl wallpaper
papier préencollé	ready-pasted wallpaper
revêtement mural	wall covering
toile de verre (f)	glass fibre wall covering

Les textiles muraux – wall textiles

Instead of wallpaper, you could decorate your walls with *tissu* (cloth) or *textile mural* (wall textile). If these are natural fibres, e.g. cotton or silk, the sheets must be fitted onto battens, with a polystyrene or other thick liner. Synthetics can also be hung this way, but can also be pasted onto the wall.

coton (m)	cotton
laine (f)	wool
lin (m)	linen
molleton (m)	flannel/felt
soie (f)	silk
tissu (m)	fabric covering
toile de jute (f)	hessian
velour (m)	velvet

Les outils – tools

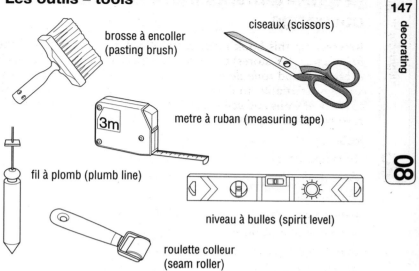

brosse à encoller
(pasting brush)

ciseaux (scissors)

metre à ruban (measuring tape)

fil à plomb (plumb line)

niveau à bulles (spirit level)

roulette colleur
(seam roller)

brosse (f) à encoller	pasting brush
brosse à maroufler	wallpaper brush
brosse d'encollage	pasting brush
ciseaux (m)	scissors
couteau à lame	Stanley knife, or similar
couteau à reboucher	filling knife
couteau universel	alternative name for Stanley knife
décolleuse (f)	paper stripper
éponge (f)	sponge
époussette (f)	wallpaper smoother
ficelle (f)	string
fil (m) à plomb	plumb line
mètre (m) à ruban	measuring tape
niveau (m) à bulles	spirit level
roulette (f) colleur	seam roller
roulette à joint	seam roller
table à encoller	pasting table

Le carrelage – tiling

There are two French words that translate to tile, but they refer to different types of material:

- *un carreau* is the word when you mean a (ceramic) wall or floor tile

- *une dalle* is the word for other sorts of tiles, e.g. cork tiles, mirror tiles – it also means flagstone or paving slab.

But just to confuse matters, a vinyl (floor) tile can be *un carreau en vinyl* or *une dalle vinyl*.

Floor tile quality

There are two standard ways for describing the quality of floor tiles. The first is simply a measure of 'toughness', and tiles are graded 1 to 4 (4 = toughest). The second and more sophisticated way uses the *UPEC* scale:

U *usure* – resistance to general wear

P *poinçonnement* – resistance to impacts, e.g. from furniture legs or high heels

E *eau* – water resistance

C *chimique* – chemical resistance

For example, a tile rated *U2 P2 E3 C1* is reasonably tough and water resistant and suitable for bathrooms; for patios, a tile rated *U4 P3 E3 C1* offers higher wear and impact resistance.

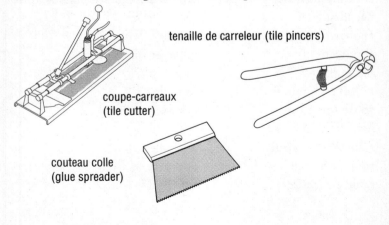

tenaille de carreleur (tile pincers)

coupe-carreaux
(tile cutter)

couteau colle
(glue spreader)

carreau (m)	tile
carreau (m) au mur	wall tile
carreau en faïence	ceramic tile
carrelage mural	wall tiling
carreau (m) par terre	floor tile
carrelette (f)	tile cutter
colle à carrelage	tile cement
coupe-carreaux (m)	tile cutter
couteau colle	glue spreader
dalle de mirroir	mirror tile
dalle liege	cork tile
plaquette de parement	facing panels (imitation brick, etc.)
tenaille de carreleur	tile pincers

Les revêtements sols – floor coverings

The French simply do not use carpets and vinyls as much as we do, so don't expect to find the same choices or the same prices. They have gone for wood laminates in a big way, just as we have in the UK, so there's plenty of those around. But the traditional French house has tiled floors in the kitchen, bathroom, conservatory and similar hard-worn places, and a lot of solid parquet elsewhere. Learn from the locals. They have been living with their climate all their lives. Bare tiled and wood floor are cooler in the summer and easy to keep clean all year round.

moquette (f)	carpet, just in case you want it
parquet (m)	wood flooring (solid or laminates)
parquet à cliquer	click-together laminate
parquet à clouer	wood floor, fastened by nails
parquet de bois massif	solid wood flooring
sol (m) stratifié	laminate flooring
sol vinylique	vinyl flooring
tapis (m)	rug

Les rideaux et les stores – curtains and blinds

If you have shutters, you don't need any curtains, except perhaps net ones to give you some privacy when the shutters and windows are open – though that doesn't mean that you can't have them if you want them. They can be a key part of a decorative scheme, and can improve the acoustics of a room.

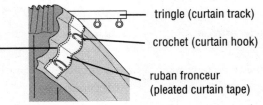

tringle (curtain track)

tête de rideau
(heading)

crochet (curtain hook)

ruban fronceur
(pleated curtain tape)

Inward-opening windows may make it difficult to hang curtains, but they make it almost impossible to fit blinds across the whole aperture. The simple solution is to fit blinds directly to the windows.

cantonnière (f)	curtain pelmet
crochet (m)	curtain hook
ruban fronceur	curtain tape
store (m)	blind
store vénitien	Venetian blind
tête de rideau	heading
tête flamande	high heading that conceals track
tringle (f) à rideaux	curtain track
tringle chemin de fer	metal curtain track
tringle ronde	curtain rod
voile (m)	netting
voilage (m)	net curtains

Les meubles – furniture

Le séjour et la salle à manger – the living room and dining room

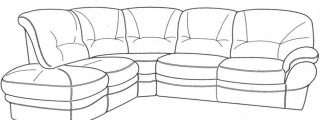

canapé (sofa)

cabriolet (low back armchair)

banquette-lit (sofa-bed)

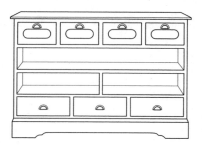

serviteur (dresser)

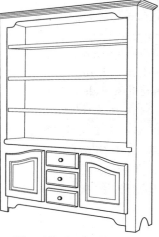

bibus (display/storage cabinet with open shelves)

La chambre – the bedroom

commode (chest of drawers)

lampe de chevet
(bedside light)

couette (duvet)

table de chevet
(bedside cabinet)

lit (bed)

mezzanine (raised bed)

coffre (chest)

argentier (m)	part-glazed cabinet, originally for silverware (argent = silver)
armoire (f)	wardrobe or large cupboard
armoirette (f)	small cupboard
baldaquin (m)	canopy, *lit à baldaquin* = four-poster bed
banc (m)	bench
banc du lit (m)	low bench in bedroom
banquette (f) lit	sofa-bed

bibliothèque (f)	bookcase
bibus (m)	display/storage cabinet with open shelves
bonnetière (f)	tall slim cupboard, originally for bonnets
buffet (m)	sideboard
cabriolet (m)	armchair (low back, round)
caisson (m)	small cabinet
canapé (m)	sofa
canné	cane, rattan
chaise (f)	chair
chiffonnier (m)	tall set of drawers
coffre (m)	chest
coiffeuse (f)	dressing table
colonne (f)	'column' – set of shelves and cupboards
commode (f)	chest of drawers
couette (f)	duvet
dressoir (m)	dresser
fauteuil (m)	easy chair
lampe (f) de chevet	bedside light
lit (m)	bed
lot (m)...	set of, e.g. *le lot 2 tiroirs* = set of 2 drawers
matelas (m)	mattress
meuble (m) de drapier	standing set of shelves
meuble d'entrée	small cupboard, typically placed by entrance door
meuble hi-fi	hi-fi cabinet
mezzanine (f)	raised bed
oreiller (m)	pillow
rayonnage (m)	set of shelves
serviteur (m)	dining room cupboard/dresser
siège (m)	seat
sièges de complément	easy chairs and sofas

table (f)	table
table (f) basse	coffee table
table de chevet (m)	bedside cabinet
vitrine (f)	showcase

English–French quick reference

La peinture – paint

brush	brosse (f), pinceau (m)
dust sheet	bâche (f)
gloss	brillant
masking tape	ruban (m) de masquage
masonry paint	peinture façade
non-drip	anti-goutte
one-coat	monocouche
paint tray	bac à peinture
paper towel	chiffon (m)
primer	peinture d'impression
roller	rouleau (m)
undercoat	apprêt (m), sous-couche (f)
turpentine	térébenthine (f)
varnish	vernis (m)
wood stain	lasure (f), teinture (f)

Les revêtements muraux – wall coverings

cork tile	dalle (f) de liège
filling knife	couteau à reboucher
lining paper	papier peint à peindre
measuring tape	mètre (m) à ruban
paper stripper	décolleuse (f)
pasting brush	brosse (f) à encoller
pasting table	table à encoller
plumb line	fil (m) à plomb
scissors	ciseaux (m)

seam roller	roulette (f) colleur, roulette à joint
spirit level	niveau (m) à bulles
sponge	éponge (f)
Stanley knife	couteau à lame, couteau universal
string	ficelle (f)
textile, for walls	textile mural, tissu (m)
vinyl wallpaper	papier peint vinyl
wallpaper	papier peint
wallpaper brush	brosse à maroufler
wallpaper paste	colle murale (f)
wallpaper, ready-pasted	papier préencollé
wallpaper smoother	époussette (f)

Le carrelage – tiling

ceramic tile	carreau en faïence
facing panels	plaquette de parement
floor tile	carreau (m) par terre
glue spreader	couteau colle
mirror tile	dalle de mirroir
tile	carreau (m)
tile cement	colle à carrelage
tile cutter	carrelette (f), coupe-carreaux (m)
tile pincers	tenaille de carreleur
wall tile	carreau (m) au mur

Les revêtements sols – floor coverings

carpet	moquette (f)
laminate flooring	sol (m) stratifié
nailed wood floor	parquet à clouer
rug	tapis (m)
solid wood flooring	parquet de bois massif
vinyl flooring	sol vinylique
wood flooring	parquet

Les rideaux et les stores – curtains and blinds

blind	store (m)
curtain	rideau (m)
curtain hook	crochet (m)
curtain pelmet	cantonnière (f)
curtain rod	tringle ronde
curtain tape	ruban fronceur
curtain track	tringle (f) à rideaux
curtain track, metal	tringle chemin de fer
heading (of curtain)	tête de rideau
net curtains	voilage (m)
Venetian blind	store vénitien

Les meubles – furniture

armchair	cabriolet (m)
bed	lit (m)
bedside cabinet	table de chevet (m)
bedside light	lampe (f) de chevet
bench	banc (m)
bookcase	bibliothèque (f)
chair	chaise (f)
chest	coffre (m)
chest of drawers	commode (f)
coffee table	table (f) basse
cupboard	armoire (f), placard (m)
cupboard, small	amoirette (f)
dresser	dressoir (m), serviteur (m)
dressing table	coiffeuse (f)
duvet	couette (f)
easy chair	fauteuil (m)
hi-fi cabinet	meuble hi-fi
low bench for bedroom	banc de lit (m)
mattress	matelas (m)
pillow	oreiller (m)

seat	siège (m)
set of shelves	rayonnage (m)
sideboard	buffet (m)
sofa	canapé (m)
sofa-bed	banquette (f) lit
table	table (f)
video cabinet	meuble vidéo
wardrobe	armoire (f)

09

le jardin – the garden

Almost the same...

It may be obvious, but it's still worth saying. Once you get south of the Loire, you are into a different climate, a different eco-system – and a different approach to gardens.

The lawn is generally the centre of a British garden, but once you get south of the Loire, in most places it's too hot and dry to keep a lawn green through the summer without regular watering. If you don't have your own spring or well to draw from, you'll have to pay every time you use the *arroseur* (sprinkler) – if you are allowed to use it. They have hosepipe bans in France as well, at times. And will you be there to water it and cut it? If not, who is going to be there to look after it for you, and at what cost?

What's the temperature range in your area? We have long hot summers down in Lot et Garonne, but in January when the wind blows out from the cold heart of Europe, it's warmer in Southampton. Tender plants can get wiped out, ponds and pools can suffer if the really cold weather lasts for more than a few days.

Peer over the fence and see how your neighbours use their gardens. What are they growing? And why? In the countryside, the French tend to use at least part of their garden area for fruit, vegetables and herbs – the sensible approach that you'd expect from a nation that loves its food. Should you do this? Can you do this? Are you there throughout the growing season to water and weed?

For most Brits in France, the most important parts of the garden are not the lawn and the veg plot, but the swimming pool and the patio. Lazy afternoons by the pool and summer evenings sipping wine and eating olives on the patio with friends. Isn't that why you bought the house?

Check at the mairie

◆ Walls and fences may be subject to planning controls. If you want to build a substantial one, you may need approval.

◆ A swimming pool may also need planning approval – and will certainly increase your local taxes.

Les clôtures – walls, fences and hedges

Une clôture is any kind of enclosure – fence, wall, hedge or whatever. As a general rule, you can create any kind of *clôture* up to 2 m high without planning permission, but there are exceptions.

- In some parts of the countryside – especially the more picturesque parts – *clôtures* of any type may be banned. Even where they are not banned, you will find that houses in farmland or open country, rarely have much more than a few strands of wire to keep out stray animals. You don't need walls for privacy if your nearest neighbours are the other side of the hill!

- In towns, the *mur mitoyen* (party wall) between gardens may not be more than 2.6 m high in a town of under 50,000 inhabitants, or 3.2 m high in bigger towns, and don't ask why! All party walls are a joint responsibility, by agreement – which means that if you want to replace the sagging plastic mesh by a nice new brick wall, and your neighbours are happy with the mesh, then don't expect them to split the cost.

- A *haie* (hedge) may not be planted closer than half a metre from the boundary of the plot – so it doesn't overhang when grown. Similarly, trees may not be planted closer than 2 m.

If you want to build a new *clôture*, the best way to start – as always – is to look around you. What do the locals have around their properties? Would this suit you? If so, you can almost certainly go ahead without worrying. If you want to build something that is very different, go and talk to the mairie first.

clôture (f) croisée	fence of diagonally crossed lathes
clôture lame	picket fence – low fence of wooden rails
clôture treillis soudés	welded wire mesh fence
grillage (m)	mesh fencing
lisse (f)	rail of fence
natte brise-vue (f)	mesh privacy screen
panneau (m) claustra	fencing panel
portail (m)	gate
poteau (m)	fence post

Les dépendances – outbuildings

When planning outbuildings, remember that if they are more than 2 m² or 1.5 m high – i.e. anything more than a big dog kennel or a small tool store – permission is needed. You must submit a déclaration de travaux (notice of works), and you may even need a permis de construire (building permit).

La piscine – the swimming pool

For many people, a swimming pool is an essential part of any holiday in the sun. Installing one is quite simple – just decide how big it should be, where it should go and how much you are willing to pay and get a professional to do the job! It won't be cheap – expect to pay at least €15,000 for a decent-sized pool – and it will need regular maintenance, which will take time and money. But the pool will add value to the house, if you ever come to resell it, and you cannot put a price on the pleasure it will give to you and your guests.

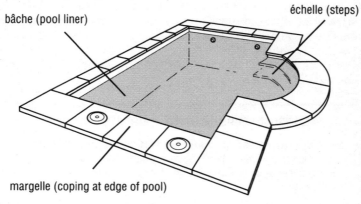

bâche (pool liner)

échelle (steps)

margelle (coping at edge of pool)

Some things to consider when planning your pool – discuss these with the pool builder:

- Should you opt for a salt water pool? Salt water discourages algae and needs lower chlorine levels.

- What kind of summer and winter covers will the pool need? Wide and/or unusual shaped pools need big covers, and these can be very heavy to roll up or out again. Can whoever will be at the house manage the pool covers if need be?

- Where will the pump and filtration unit go? Is there a convenient place in the outbuildings or do you need a pump house?

Your new swimming pool may be subject to planning controls – it depends upon the size and type.

- A covered swimming pool is subject to the same controls as any other building – you would normally have to obtain a *permis de construire* (planning permission, see Chapter 3).

- An open swimming pool would normally be subject to the *déclaration de travaux* (notice of works, Chapter 3) process. In practice, an open pool of under 100 m² will usually be nodded through without formalities.

- Above ground, removable, pools of less than 20 m² and less than 1m high are not subject to any controls.

If you get your pool builders involved early in the process, they can guide you through the paperwork, or handle it for you.

If you construct a fixed pool, you must inform the local *centre des impôts* (tax office), as it will affect your *taxe d'habitation* and *taxe foncière* (local property taxes, see Chapter 2). Don't forget to do this. Aerial photography makes it very simple for *communes* to keep track of pools, and they can get quite stroppy with people who have not declared new ones!

Clôture de sécurité – safety barrier

By law, all swimming pools (except for above-ground models) in rented properties must have a child safety barrier. If you intend to rent your house, work a barrier into the initial design and costings.

bâche (f)	pool liner
barrière (f)	safety fence
bassin (m) préformé	moulded pool liner
chlore (m)	chlorine
clôture de sécurité	safety barrier
coque (f) de piscine	moulded pool liner

couverture (f)	cover
échelle (f)	steps
feutre (m)	underlay for liner
filtre (m) à sable	sand filter
margelle (f)	coping (for edge of pool)
piscine hors sol	above ground pool
pompe (f)	pump
robot (m) pour piscine	pool cleaning robot
terrasse (f) bois	decking
traitement (m)	treatment

Pool robots come in weird and wonderful shapes, but all work in much the same way. They are powered by the main pump and wander across the bottom and up the sides, dislodging and hoovering up sediment.

Le mobilier de jardin – garden

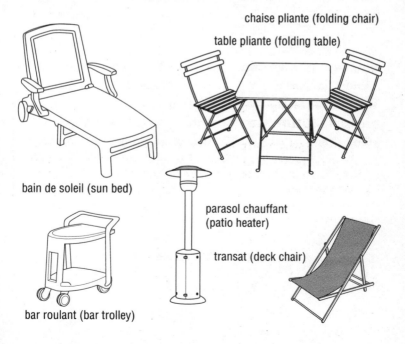

chaise pliante (folding chair)

table pliante (folding table)

bain de soleil (sun bed)

parasol chauffant
(patio heater)

transat (deck chair)

bar roulant (bar trolley)

furniture

bac (m) à sable	sand pit
bain (m) de soleil	sun bed
balancelle (f)	swing seat
bar (m) roulant	bar trolley
barbecue (m)	barbeque
borne (f) d'allée	garden light, usually on a short pole intended for use by paths or ponds – literally 'edge of path'
chaise (f) pliante	folding chair
coussin (m)	cushion
fauteuil (m) pliant	folding armchair
fonte alu	cast aluminium
housse (f)	cover for furniture, typically of clear or coloured plastic
lanterne (f) à détecteur	security light
matelas (m)	mattress (for sun bed)
parasol (m)	parasol, with own stand or to set into a table
parasol chauffant	patio heater
projecteur (f) à détecteur	security floodlight
séchoir (m) jardin	rotary clothes dryer
store (m) de façade	sun blind
torche (f)	flare
transat (m)	deckchair, from '*transatlantique*' – the liners on whose decks they were first used

borne d'allée (garden light) – and remember that solar powered ones work very well in the French climate

Le jardinage – gardening

Garden centres are not as common in France as they are in the UK – the French have not in the past shared our obsession with lawns and borders, although they are now heading that way and *jardineries* (garden centres) do exist. However, you should have no difficulty in finding plants and seeds, pots, composts, tools and all the other necessities of gardening as there are lots of other possible sources.

* The larger *bricolages* (DIY stores) usually have a gardening section.

* In rural areas there are agricultural retailers who also handle gardening supplies. These can be very good value.

* *Maraîchers* (plant breeders) – again, mainly in rural areas – raise vegetable and flower plants from seed and sell them at the planting out stage. This is more often a farmer's sideline than a separate business. Look out for them at your local markets – it's where I head first (there's a very good market in Miramont de Guyenne every Monday).

* If you want trees and shrubs, the *pépiniériste* (nurseryman) is the specialist.

L'herbe and herbs

L'herbe is 'grass'. It can also mean 'herb', but is rarely used as such. The French normally speak of *herbes aromatiques* or *herbes médicinales* or *herbes potagères*, depending on whether they are aromatic, medicinal or for the cooking pot.

aneth (m)	dill
basilic (m)	basil
cerfeuil (m)	chervil
ciboule (f)	chives
coriandre (f)	coriander
fenouils (m)	fennel
marjolaine (f)	marjoram
menthe (f)	mint
persil (m)	parsley
thym (m)	thyme

Les outils et l'équip – tools and equipment

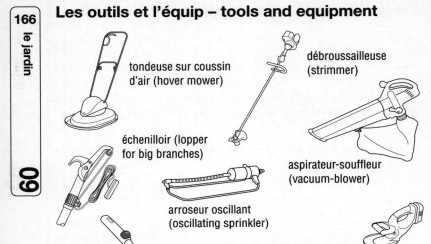

tondeuse sur coussin
d'air (hover mower)

débroussailleuse
(strimmer)

échenilloir (lopper
for big branches)

aspirateur-souffleur
(vacuum-blower)

arroseur oscillant
(oscillating sprinkler)

taille-haie (hedge trimmer)

balai à dents plates
(lawn rake)

cisaille à gazon (grass shears)

abri-bûches (m)	log shelter
abri (m) de jardin	garden shed
arrosage (m)	watering, irrigation
arroseur oscillant	oscillating sprinkler
aspirateur-souffleur (m)	vacuum-blower
balai à dents plates	lawn rake
balai cantonnier	garden brush (literally road-sweeper's brush)
bêche (f)	spade
brouette (f)	wheelbarrow
broyeur (m)	shredder
chevalet (m) de sciage	sawhorse
cisaille à gazon	grass shears
cisaille à haies	hedge shears
coffre (m) de rangement	storage chest
coupe-bordures (m)	border trimmer

coupe-branches	branch lopper
cuve (f)	water barrel
débroussailleuse (f)	strimmer
déplantoir (m)	potting trowel
dévidoir (m)	roller for hosepipe
ébrancheur	branch lopper
échenilloir	lopper for big branches
engrais (m)	fertiliser
fontaine (f)	fountain
fourche (f) à bêcher	gardening fork (*à bêcher* means 'for digging')
gazon (m)	lawn
graines (f)	seeds
griffe (f) de jardin	claw
incinérateur (m)	incinerator
pot (m) de fleurs	flowerpot
rallonge électrique (f)	extension lead
râteau (m)	rake
réservoir (m)	tank
sac (m) poubelle	rubbish bag
scarificateur (m)	scarifier for lawn
scie à bûches	log saw
sécateur (m) de jardin	secateur
serre (f)	greenhouse
taille-haie (m)	hedge trimmer
taille-herbe (m)	grass cutter
terreau (m)	potting compost
tondeuse (f)	mower
tondeuse autoportée	ride-on mower
tondeuse sur coussin d'air	hover mower
transplantoir (m)	potting trowel
tronçonneuse (f)	chainsaw
tuyau (m)	hose

English–French quick reference

Walls, fences and hedges – les clôtures

fence	clôture
fence post	poteau (m)
fence rail	lisse (f)
fencing panel	panneau (m) claustra
gate	portail (m)
hedge	haie (f)
mesh fencing	grillage (m)
wall	mur (m)

Swimming pool – la piscine

chlorine	chlore (m)
coping (for edge of pool)	margelle (f)
cover	couverture (f)
decking	terrasse (f) bois
pool liner, moulded	bassin (m) préformé, coque (f)
pool liner, sheet	bâche (f)
pump	pompe (f)
safety fence	clôture de sécurité
sand filter	filtre (m) à sable
steps	échelle (f)

Le mobilier de jardin – garden furniture

bar trolley	bar (m) roulant
cast aluminium	fonte alu
chair with arms	fauteuil (m)
cover for furniture	housse (f)
cushion	coussin (m)
deckchair	transat (m)
flare	torche (f)
floodlight	projecteur (f)
folding	pliant

garden light	borne (f) d'allée
mattress (for sun bed)	matelas (m)
patio heater	parasol chauffant
rotary clothes dryer	séchoir (m) jardin
sand pit	bac (m) à sable
security light	lanterne (f) à détecteur
sun bed	bain (m) de soleil
sun blind	store (m) de façade
swing seat	balancelle (f)

Les herbes potagères – cooking herbs

basil	basilic (m)
chervil	cerfeuil (m)
chives	ciboule (f)
coriander	coriandre (f)
dill	aneth (m)
fennel	fenouils (m)
marjoram	marjolaine (f)
mint	menthe (f)
parsley	persil (m)
thyme	thym (m)

Le jardinage – gardening

branch lopper	ébrancheur, échenilloir
claw	griffe (f) de jardin
extension lead	rallonge électrique (f)
fertiliser	engrais (m)
flowerpot	pot (m) de fleurs
fountain	fontaine (f)
garden brush	balai cantonnier
garden shed	abri (m) de jardin
gardening fork	fourche (f) à bêcher
grass cutter	taille-herbe (m)
greenhouse	serre (f)

hedge trimmer	taille-haie (m)
hose	tuyau (m)
hover mower	tondeuse sur coussin d'air
incinerator	incinérateur (m)
lawn	gazon (m)
lawn rake	balai à dents plates
log saw	scie à bûches
log shelter	abri-bûches (m)
mower	tondeuse (f)
potting trowel	déplantoir
rake	râteau (m)
ride-on mower	tondeuse autoportée
roller for hosepipe	dévidoir (m)
rubbish bag	sac (m) poubelle
sawhorse	chevalet (m) de sciage
seeds	graines (f)
shears	cisaille (f)
shredder	broyeur (m)
spade	bêche (f)
sprinkler, oscillating	arroseur (m) oscillant
storage chest	coffre (m) de rangement
strimmer	débroussailleuse (f)
vacuum-blower	aspirateur-souffleur (m)
water barrel	cuve (f)
wheelbarrow	brouette (f)

10

une heure de français – an hour of French

The CD and the book

This chapter and the CD are built around the same sets of words, and should be used together. The CD gives practice in speaking and listening; the book links the written word to the spoken word.

The aim of this chapter is not to teach you French – if you want to learn the language properly, try a *Michel Thomas* course, or one of the titles in the *Teach Yourself* series, such as *French* or *Instant French*. The aim here is to provide you with a core of words and phrases that will help you to find what you need when you are buying, building, maintaining or equipping your French home.

If you already speak French to a greater or less degree, we hope that this chapter will give you a firmer grasp of those specialist words that the householder needs. Skip the rest of this section and go straight to *La recherche – the search* (page 180) and Track 2 on the CD.

Speaking and listening

When you speak French to a native, don't try too hard to get a perfect accent. If the French think that you can speak their language well, they won't make allowance when they talk to you. And you need them to make allowances! French people tend to talk quickly – you need them to slow down so that you can distinguish each word or phrase from the next. You rehearse what you want to say in your head, let it flow out smoothly, then stand there like an idiot after they reply, without a clue as to what they said. I've done this too often myself!

Speak slowly yourself, and let them hear from your accent that you are a foreigner, and they might speak more slowly and clearly to you. If necessary, ask them to slow down.

Here's your first – and most essential – French phrase:

encore et plus lentement   again and more slowly

To which you could add, politely:

s'il vous plaît   please, literally 'if it pleases you'

What follows is a brief guide to basic pronunciation. Listen to the CD while you are working through this.

Lost consonants

The French do not pronounce every letter. *h* is always silent and they usually drop the last letter of words ending in *r*, *t*, *s*, *x* or *z*.

French	sounds like	means
bas	**bah**	low
haut	**oh**	high
trés	**tray**	very
payer	**payay**	to pay
vous	**voo**	you

But if the next word starts with a vowel, the consonant is pronounced.

vous avez	**voos avay**	you have

A final *e* is only said if it has an accent (*é*) or if it's the only vowel in the word.

poste	**post**	post office
homme	**om**	man
de	**de** (as in 'the')	of
passé	**passay**	past

Other consonants

Most are pronounced as in English. These aren't.

c is **k** if followed by *a*, *o* or *u*

cuisine	**kwizine**	kitchen

c is **s** if followed by *e* or *i*, or if it has a cedilla accent *ç*

cent	**sent**	hundred
maçon	**masson**	builder

ch is **sh**

chez	**shay**	at the house of

j like the **g** in mirage

joli	**jolly**	pretty

qu is **k** not **kw** as in English

qui	**kee**	who

Vowels

First, the vowels by themselves:

a is generally **a** as in **had**

à la place	**a la plass**	to the place

e   is **e** as in y**e**s, but *é* is **ay** as in h**ay**. *er*, *et*, *ez* are pronounced **ay** at the ends of words

| *venir* | **veneer** | to come |
| *venez-vous* | **venay voo** | are you coming? |

i   is **i** as in f**i**x

| *dix* | **dis** | ten |

o   is **o** as in p**o**t

| *porte* | **porte** | door |

u   is somewhere between **oo** as in m**oo** and **iew** as in v**iew**

| *la rue* | **la riew** | the road |

Now some combinations that produce a single sound:

ai   is like the English **ai** as in pl**ai**ce

| *maison* | **maizon** | house |

au or *eau* is **au** as in **Au**gust

| *au marché* | **au marshay** | to the market |
| *beau* | **bau** | beautiful |

ou is **oo** as in wh**oo**

| *l'égout* | **legoo** | the drains |

oi is **wa** as in **wa**gwam

| *chèz moi* | **shay mwa** | my house |

ui   is **wee** as in **wee**k

| *je suis* | **juh swee** | I am |

an, *on* and *en* have the same nasal **on** as in Dij**on**

le banc	**le bonk**	the bank
l'enfant	**lonfon**	the child
bon	**bon**	good

Gender and endings

All nouns are either masculine or feminine. I've never understood why or what determines the gender of a noun (apart from the obvious ones that refer to people or animals). One that ends in 'e' is almost certainly feminine, as are most words ending in 'tion', but that leaves an awful lot that you just have to know.

A noun's gender affects the words around it. For 'the' you use *le* if the noun is masculine and *la* if it is feminine; likewise 'a' is either *un* (m) or *une* (f). But if there's more than one of them, it's always the same *les* (the) or *des* (some).

For example, *maison* (house) is feminine, and *manoir* (manor house) is masculine. That gives us:

the house	*la maison*
the manor	*le manoir*
a house	*une maison*
a manor	*un manoir*
the houses	*les maisons*
some manors	*des manoirs*

I try not to get too hung up on the gender thing. If you talk about *le maison*, instead of *la maison*, a French person will know what you mean, though they may shrug and think '*rosbif*!'

Adjectives have a different ending if a noun is feminine. Usually, it's just a matter of adding *e* to the end. For example, *grand* means 'big', so 'a big house' – which is feminine – becomes *une grande maison* or *une maison grande*. (The adjective is often placed after the noun.) The added *e* can change the sound of a word. For example, in *petit* (small), the last *t* is not pronounced, but in *petite* the *t* is sounded.

Sometimes the change of ending is more than just an added *e*, but we're not going to worry about that here.

The endings of adjectives also change with plural nouns – and usually by just adding an *s* to the end, to match the *s* on the end of the noun.

a small house	*une petite maison*
the big manor	*le grand manoir*
the big houses	*les grandes maisons*

Verbs

French verbs 'conjugate'. Their endings, and sometimes the whole word, change depending upon who is doing the thing and when they are doing it. Verbs also conjugate in English, but not as much. However, there's a bright side – as the endings of words are often not pronounced, they may be spelled differently but sound the same.

For example, *aimer* means 'to like'. Here's how it conjugates:

j'aime	**jaim**	I like
tu aimes	**too aim**	you like
il aime	**il aim**	he likes
elle aime	**el aim**	she likes
nous aimons	**noos aimon**	we like
vous aimez	**voos aimay**	you like
ils aiment	**eels aim**	they like

Notice that the verb sounds the same for all of them, apart from *nous aimons* and *vous aimez*. That makes life simple, and in practice if you said *vous aim* to a French seller, they would know what you meant well enough to sell you stuff.

Most other verbs that end *er* conjugate in the same way, so to say these, just chop off the *er* or add *ons* or *ez* if you want the 'we' or 'you' form. e.g. with *demander* (to ask), you would say *je demand* (I ask) or *nous demandons* (we ask).

Other verbs end in *re* or *ir*. Likewise with these, trim the verb down to its core and add *ons* or *ez* if needed. *Venir* is to come, which gives us *nous venons* (we are coming).

Some verbs change more, and you should at least be aware of these two:

être – **to be**

je suis	**je swee**	I am
tu es	**too eh**	you are
il/elle est	**il/el eh**	he/she is
nous sommes	**noo som**	we are
vous êtes	**voos et**	you are
ils/elles sont	**il/el son**	they are

avoir – **to have**

j'ai	**jay**	I have
tu as	**too a**	you have
il/elle a	**il/el a**	he/she has
nous avons	**noos avon**	we have
vous avez	**voos avay**	you have
ils ont	**ils on**	they have

We've only looked at the present tense. There are also several ways of talking about past and future events, all of which affect the shape and sound of the verb. And there is no single pattern to the way they conjugate, even for the 'regular' verbs – there around 80 patterns and permutations in total. Take my advice, live in the present, never write anything down, and just chop off the ending of the verb and add *ons* if its *nous* and *ez* if its *vous*. If nothing else, you will amuse the locals, and when they've stopped laughing, they'll be pleased to help you.

Tu et vous – which you?

The French have two words for 'you'. Vous is the plural and is also used when speaking to someone to show respect. Tu is the singular form, but should only be used when speaking to a child or a friend. It's rude to tutoyer someone (use tu instead of vous) if you are not familiar with them.

---

ne...pas – not

To say 'not' you need two words: *ne* goes before the verb and *pas* goes after it. For example:

I am not…   je ne suis pas…

Here's a 'not' phrase you may find very useful:

I do not understand   je ne comprends pas

If you want to say 'not' without a verb, just use *pas*:

not today   pas aujourd'hui

Greetings

hello, literally 'good day'	bonjour
good evening	bonsoir
goodbye	au revoir
have a good day	bonne journée
thank you	merci
thank you very much	merci beaucoup
don't mention it	je vous en prie
pardon me	excusez-moi

how do you do?	comment ça va?
fine, thanks	bien, merci
I am called…	je m'appelle…

Asking questions

You can form questions in three ways. Either switch the noun-verb order, so that you start with the verb, e.g.

| do you speak English? | parlez-vous anglais? |

Or start with the phrase *est-ce que…*(is it that), then use the normal word order:

est-ce que vous parlez anglais?

Or say it as if it was a statement, but with an inflection:

vous parlez anglais?

qui (who), *où* (where), *quel* or *quelle* (what), *quand* (when) and *pourquoi* (why) questions use the same order as in English.

where is the town hall?	où est la mairie?
it's to the right	c'est à droite
it's to the left	c'est à gauche
it's straight on	c'est tout droit

Les nombres – numbers

0	zéro	13	treize	31	trente et un
1	un, une	14	quatorze	32	trente deux
2	deux	15	quinze	40	quarante
3	trois	16	seize	50	cinquante
4	quatre	17	dix-sept	60	soixante
5	cinq	18	dix-huit	70	soixante-dix
6	six	19	dix-neuf	80	quatre-vingts
7	sept	20	vingt	90	quatre-vingt-dix
8	huit	21	vingt et un	100	cent
9	neuf	22	vingt-deux	200	deux cents
10	dix	23	vingt-trois	1000	mille
11	onze	etc		2 000	deux mille
12	douze	30	trente	1 000 000	un million

it's over there	c'est par là
it's here	c'est ici
it's how much?	c'est combien?
why?	pourquoi?
this house is cheap, why?	cette maison est un petit prix, pourquoi?
why is this house so dear?	cette maison est si chère, pourquoi?
how old is this house?	quel âge a cette maison?
what time is it?	quelle heure est-il?
it is 7 o'clock	il est sept heures
half past eight	huit heures et demie
quarter to ten	dix heures moins le quart
at 15.00	à quinze heures
(They normally use the 24-hour clock.)	
it's lunch time	c'est l'heure du déjeuner
when?, at what time?	à quelle heure?
what day?	quel jour?
what date?	quelle date?
can we set a date?	pouvons-nous fixer une date?

Les dates – dates

Les jours – the days

Sunday	dimanche
Monday	lundi
Tuesday	mardi
Wednesday	mercredi
Thursday	jeudi
Friday	vendredi
Saturday	samedi
tomorrow	demain
today	aujourd'hui
yesterday	hier

Les mois – the months

January	janvier
February	février
March	mars
April	avril
May	mai
June	juin
July	juillet
August	août
September	septembre
October	octobre
November	novembre
December	december

La recherche – the search (Track 2)

Let's start with some words and phrases to help you find that house.

I am looking for...	je cherche...
we are looking for...	nous cherchons...
I want to buy...	je veux acheter...
we want to buy...	nous voulons acheter...
...a little house	...une petite maison
...a large house	...une grande maison
...a flat	...un appartement
...in the country	...de campagne
...in the town	...une maison de bourg
...to restore	...à rénover
...in good condition	...en bon état
is this house for sale?	cette maison est à vendre?

Defining the house

Three key ways to define a house are its size – measured in square metres of floor space – the number of rooms and its price. You'll need to brush up your numbers for all of these. But if you want to make sure that you've understood the numbers correctly, ask the agent to write them down. Figures don't need translation!

about	environ
more than	plus de
less than	moins de
50 m² (cottage size)	cinquante mètres carrés
100 m² (average UK semi)	cent mètres carrés
200 m² (large detached)	deux cents mètres carrés
two bedrooms	deux chambres
five rooms	cinq pièces
€60 000	soixante mille euros
€120 000	cent vingt mille euros
€1 000 000	un million d'euros

The features

What features are essential, desirable or to be avoided?

there must be…	il faut…
is there…	est-ce qu'il y a…
…the possibility of…	…la possibilité de…
…a kitchen	…une cuisine
…a bathroom	…une salle de bains
…a swimming pool	…une piscine
…a garden	…un jardin
…a convertible attic	…un grenier aménageable
…a cellar	…une cave
…a beautiful view	…une belle vue
…work to be done	…travaux à prévoir
is it on the mains drains?	est-elle tout à l'égout?
is the roof in a good state?	le toit est en bon état?

Your decision

And what do you think of the property? Do you want to keep looking or is it time to start negotiating the price?

no, thank you	non, merci
it's too dear	c'est trop cher
it's too big/small	c'est trop grand/petit
there is too much to do	il y a trop à faire
perhaps	peut-être
I have other houses to see	j'ai d'autres maisons à voir
do you have other houses?	avez-vous d'autres maisons?
I like this house…	j'aime cette maison…
we like this house…	nous aimons cette maison…
…but not the price	…mais pas le prix
can we negotiate?	pouvons-nous négocier?
here is my offer	voici mon offre
it's perfect!	c'est parfait!
agreed	d'accord

La vente – the sale (Track 3)

There is not enough in this book to enable you to handle safely the legal and financial aspects of house purchase. You must have a good grasp of French – and of French law – or the services of a translator and/or English-speaking lawyer.

Before you commit yourself to the purchase, you may want to check the price, or the cost – and feasibility – of essential works.

could you recommend...	pouvez-vous recommander...
...a valuer	...un expert immobilier
...a master of the works	...un maître d'oeuvre
...a notary	...un notaire
I need/we need...	j'ai/nous avons besoin de...
...a valuation...	...une évaluation...
...an estimate...	...un devis...
...for this house	...pour cette maison

(There is more on estimates in the next section, *Les travaux* – building work, Track 4.)

You might want to find out the level of the local taxes and/or the service charges in an apartment block, and you should also check who's paying the agent's fees.

where is the town hall?	où est la mairie?
where is the tax office?	où est le trésor public?
how much are...?	c'est combien...?
...the taxes...	...les taxes...
...for this address	...pour cette adresse
...the service charges of l'immeuble	...les charges de services de the apartment block
who pays the agency fees?	qui paye les frais d'agence?
the seller pays	le vendeur paye

With your queries answered, you should be ready to commit, though there may be conditions in some cases.

we are ready to buy	nous sommes prêts à acheter
I want to buy this house...	je veux acheter cette maison...

…at the price of…€ 000	…au prix de…mille euros
…under these conditions	…avec ces clauses suspensives
there must be a satisfactory zoning certificate	il faut un certificat d'urbanisme satisfaisant
I must get a mortgage	je dois obtenir une hypothèque
I would like to see the health expert's certificates	je veux voir les certificats de l'expert en état sanitaire
I cannot give you the deposit today	je ne peux pas vous donner l'acompte aujourd'hui
I will transfer the money from the UK	je transfèrerait l'argent du Royaume Uni
when does the cooling-off period start?	quand commence le délai de réflexion?

If you want to clarify any points of the sale agreement, or set up a French will, you will need to visit the *notaire*.

where is the notary's office?	où est le bureau du notaire?
do you speak English?	parlez-vous anglais?
I would like to make a will	je veux faire un testament
we want joint ownership of the house	nous voulons la propriété tontine de cette maison

If they are present, get the water, gas, electricity and telephone accounts transferred to your name at the time of the sale. Ask the *agent immobilier*.

which services are present?	quels services sont là?
can you transfer the accounts to me / to us?	pouvez-vous transférer les comptes à moi / à nous?
where is the EDF office?	où est le bureau EDF?
which are the rubbish collection days?	quels sont les jours de ramassage des ordures?
where is the waste collection site?	où est la déchetterie?
where is the recycling centre?	où est le centre de recyclage?

And don't forget the *s'il vous plaît* when you ask a question, or the *merci* when you get a reply.

Les travaux – building work (Track 4)

As long as you hold your meetings on site, armed with a *croquis* (sketch) or *plan* (plan), you can get a long way with a limited vocabulary and lots of hand waving. First find your work force. Ask at the *agent immobilier* or the *mairie*.

can you recommend...	pouvez-vous recommander...
...an architect	...un architecte
...a master of the works	...un maître d'oeuvre
...a builder	...un maçon
...a (roof) carpenter	...un charpentier
...a roofer	...un couvreur
...a joiner	...un menuisier
...a plumber	...un plombier
...an electrician	...un électricien
...a plasterer	...un plâtrier
...a stonemason	...un tailleur

Then specify the job on site. Notice that the word for 'new' is *nouveau* if the noun is masculine, or *nouvelle* if it is feminine.

here are my sketch and plan	voici mon croquis et mon plan
I want...	je veux...
...to knock down the walls	...faire tomber les cloisons
...to knock down these buildings	...démolir ces dépendances out-
...to convert the attic	...aménager le grenier
...to make two rooms	...créer deux pièces
the house needs...	la maison a besoin de...
...a new roof	...un nouveau toit
...a new floor	...un nouveau plancher
I want to build...	je veux construire...
...a new bathroom	...une nouvelle salle de bains
...a new kitchen	...une nouvelle cuisine
...an extra bedroom	...une chambre de plus
...a garage	...un garage
...a swimming pool	...une piscine

this big (with gestures!)	grand comme ça
this high	de cette hauteur
can you give me an estimate for this work?	pouvez-vous me donner un devis pour ces travaux?
when could you do them?	quand pouvez-vous les faire?

Do you need planning permission or approval of the work?

can I see the POS for this address?	puis-je voir le plan d'occupation du sol pour cette adresse?
could you give me...	pouvez-vous me donner...
...the address of the consultant architect	...l'adresse de l'architecte conseil
...a form for...	...un formulaire pour...
...planning permission	...le permis de construire
...permission to demolish	...le permis de démolir
...notice of works	...la déclaration de travaux

La structure – the structure

Talking to le maçon – the builder (Track 5)

can you build...	pouvez-vous construire...
...a brick wall	...un mur de brique
...a partition wall	...une cloison
...a stone chimney	...une cheminée de pierre
...a reinforced concrete floor	...un plancher de béton armé
...a lining for this wall	...un doublage pour ce mur
can you...	pouvez-vous...
...renovate the roughcast	...rénover le crépi
...repoint the walls	...jointoyer les murs
...do half-timbered walls	...faire le colombage
...do wattle and daub	...faire le torchis
there is rising damp	il y a une infiltration
the house needs a damp course	la maison a besoin d'une barrière d'étanchéité

Finding tools and materials at the bricolage (Track 6)

where can I find...	où puis-je trouver...
...builder's tools	...les outils de maçon
...a bucket	...un seau
...a chisel	...un ciseau
...a filling knife	...un couteau à enduire
...a shavehook	...un grattoir
...a shovel	...une pelle
...a spade	...une bêche
...a spirit level	...un niveau à bulles
...a trowel	...une truelle
...breeze blocks	...des parpaings
...bricks	...des briques
...cement	...du ciment
...insulation panels	...des panneaux d'isolation
...a lintel	...un linteau
...plasterboard	...du placoplâtre
...plaster blocks	...des carreaux de plâtre
...sand	...du sable
...stones	...des pierres
...wall ties	...des ancres de mur
...wood preservative	...du xylophène
...treatment for mould	...du traitement pour le moisi
where can I hire a concrete mixer?	où puis-je louer une bétonnière?

Talking to le charpentier – the roof carpenter and le couvreur – the roofer (Track 7)

I would like...	je veux...
...to convert the attic	...aménager le grenier
...create a terrace roof	...créer une toiture-terrasse
can you build...	pouvez-vous construire...
...a dormer window	...une lucarne
...a lathe and plaster ceiling	...un plafond de lattes et enduit de plâtre

can you install…	pouvez-vous installer…
…a skylight	…un vélux
…lining felt	…de l'écran de sous-toiture
…insulation	…de l'isolation
can you renovate…	pouvez-vous rénover…
…these rafters	…ces chevrons
…the joists	…les solives
…the roof trusses	…les fermes
…the hip roof	…la croupe
…the roof timbers	…le bois de charpente
…the lathing	…le lattis
…the ridge board	…la poutre de faîtage
…the valley gutter	…le chéneau
…the flashing	…les solins
…the slate clips	…les crochets
oak or pine?	du chêne ou du pin?
a roof of…	un toit de…
…flat tiles	…tuiles plates
…curved tiles	…tuiles canal
…wood shingles	…bardeaux de bois
…roofing panels	…plaques profilées
…slates	…ardoises
…thatch	…chaume

La menuiserie – woodwork

Talking to le menuisier – the joiner (Track 8)

here, we would like…	ici, nous désirons…
…a built-in cupboard	…un placard
…a door with its frame	…une porte avec l'encadrement
…panelling	…du lambris
…three shelves	…trois étagères
…wood flooring	…du parquet
…a letter box	…une boîte aux lettres

can you make…	pouvez-vous faire…
…a french window	…une porte-fenêtre
…a skylight	…une fenêtre à tabatière
…new shutters	…des nouveaux volets
…a roller shutter	…une volet roulant
…a slatted shutter	…une persienne
…a spiral staircase	…un escalier spiral
…a new handrail	…une nouvelle main courante
…a fitted wardrobe	…un dressing
…a set of shelves	…un rayonnage

Finding materials at the bricolage (Track 9)

where can I find…	où puis-je trouver…
…chipboard	…l'aggloméré
…hardboard	…les panneaux de fibres dures
…hardwood	…le bois dur
…melamine panels	…les panneaux mélaminés
…veneer	…le placage
…plywood	…le contre-plaqué
…tongue and grooved	…le bois à rainure et languette
…veneered panels	…les panneaux plaqués
…wood panels	…les panneaux de bois
…hardware for doors	…la quincaillerie pour les portes
…bolts	…des verroux
…cylinder locks	…des serrures à cylindre
…door handles	…des poignées de porte
…hinges	…des charnières
…split hinges	…des paumelles
…strap hinges	…des pentures
…mortice locks	…des serrures encastrées
…shutter catches	…des têtes de bergère
…latches	…des loquets
…shutter fastenings	…des espagnolettes

Finding tools at the bricolage (Track 10)

where are the wood tools?	où sont les outils à bois?
do you have…	avez-vous…
…chisels	…des ciseaux
…cutters (Stanley knife)	…des couteaux universels
…drill bits	…des mèches
…electric drills	…des perceuses électriques
…electric jig saws	…des scies sauteuses
…electric screwdrivers	…des visseuses électriques
…hammers	…des marteaux
…nails	…des clous
…pincers	…des tenailles
…sandpaper	…du papier de verre
…saws	…des scies
…screws	…des vis
…screwdrivers	…des tournevis
…staple guns	…des fortes agrafeuses
…tape measures	…des mètres à ruban
…wood glue	…de la colle à bois

La plomberie – plumbing

Talking to le plombier – the plumber (Track 11)

can you install…	pouvez-vous installer…
…galvanised gutters	…des gouttières zinguées
…some copper pipes	…des tuyaux de cuivre
…a waste water system	…un réseau d'évacuation
…a new joint	…un raccord nouveau
…bathroom fittings	…des installations sanitaires
…a WC	…un WC
…a septic tank	…une fosse septique
…a soakaway	…un puits perdu
…a soil pipe	…un tuyau d'égout

where is…	où est…
…the stop cock	…le robinet d'arrêt
…the drain cock	…le vidange
…the regulator	…le détendeur
…the water meter	…le compteur d'eau
we need a drainage permit	nous avons besoin d'un permis d'assainissement
do you know someone who empties septic tanks?	connaissez-vous un vidangeur?

Shopping for bathroom and kitchen equipment (Track 11)

where can I find…	où puis-je trouver…
…basins	…des lavabos
…bathtubs	…des baignoires
…medicine cabinets	…des armoires à pharmacie
…mirrors	…des miroirs
…mixer taps	…des mélangeurs
…a plug	…une bonde
…a rubbish bin	…une poubelle
…showers	…des douches
…taps	…des robinets
…towel rails	…des porte-serviettes
…a washer	…une rondelle
…kitchen equipment	…des appareils de cuisine
…a bowl	…un bac
…a cooker hood	…une hotte aspirante
…a dishwasher	…un lave-vaisselle
…hobs	…des tables de cuisson
…kitchen sinks	…des éviers
…ovens	…des fours
…washing machines	…des machines à laver
…work surfaces	…des plans de travail
I would like a sink with two bowls and one drainer	je désire un évier avec deux bacs et un égouttoir

Finding tools at the bricolage (Track 12)

I am looking for…	je cherche…
…a spanner	…une clé
…an adjustable spanner	…une clé anglaise
…cutters (for PVC pipes)	…une pince coupante
…a hacksaw	…une scie à métaux
…a mole grip	…une pince étau
…a pipe cutter	…un coupe tube
…a soldering lamp	…une lampe à souder

Le chauffage et l'électricité – heating and electricity

Talking to le chauffagiste – the heating engineer (Track 13)

can you install…	pouvez-vous installer…
…a fireplace	…une cheminée
…a boiler	…une chaudière
…some radiators	…des radiateurs
…a stove	…un poêle
…central heating	…le chauffage central
oil-fired	à fuel domestique
gas-fired	à gaz
where can I buy…	où puis-je acheter…
…coal	…du charbon
…logs	…des bûches
…wood	…du bois
can you recommend a chimneysweep?	pouvez-vous recommander un ramoneur?

Talking to l'électricien – the electrician (Track 14)

can you rewire the house?	pouvez-vous refaire l'installation électrique?
where is/are…	où est/sont…
…the mains supply point	…le conjoncteur

...the mains switch — ...le disjoncteur de branchement

...the meter — ...le compteur

...the circuit breakers — ...les disjoncteurs

can you fit... — pouvez-vous installer...

...a socket — ...une prise

...a fuse box — ...une boîte à fusibles

...a light switch — ...un interrupteur

...a light socket — ...une douille

Shopping for les appareils électriques – electrical appliances (Track 15)

where can I find... — où puis-je trouver...

...blow heaters — ...des convecteurs soufflants

...convector heaters — ...des convecteurs électriques

...electric fires — ...des cheminées électriques

...cookers — ...des cuisinières

...DVD players — ...des lecteurs DVD

...food processors — ...des robots

...freezers — ...des congélateurs

...fridges — ...des réfrigérateurs

...kettles — ...des bouilloires

...irons — ...des fers à repasser

...telephones — ...des téléphones

...TVs — ...des téléviseurs

...flat screen TVs — ...des téléviseurs à écran plat

...vacuum cleaners — ...des aspirateurs

...light fittings — ...des luminaires

...a ceiling light — ...un plafonnier

...a bedside light — ...une lampe de chevet

...a hanging light — ...une suspension

...a lamp — ...une lampe

...a wall light — ...une applique

La décoration – decorating

Finding materials at the bricolage (Track 16)

where can I find...	où puis-je trouver...
...paint	...la peinture
...gloss paint	...la peinture brillante
...masonry paint	...la peinture façade
...non-drip paint	...la peinture anti-gouttes
...primer	...la peinture d'impression
...undercoat	...la sous-couche
...varnish	...le vernis
...wood stain	...la lasure
is this one-coat?	est-ce que c'est monocouche?
do you sell...	vendez-vous...
...wall coverings	...les revêtements muraux
...textiles, for walls	...les textiles muraux
...wallpaper	...le papier peint
...cork tiles	...les dalles de liège
...lining paper	...le papier peint à peindre
...tiles	...des carreaux
...floor tiles	...des carreaux par terre
...mirror tiles	...des dalles de miroir

Finding tools at the bricolage (Track 17)

where can I find...	où puis-je trouver...
...a measuring tape	...un mètre à ruban
...a paper stripper	...une décolleuse
...a pasting brush	...une brosse à encoller
...scissors	...des ciseaux
...a spirit level	...un niveau à bulle
...a sponge	...une éponge
...string	...de la ficelle
...wallpaper paste	...de la colle murale
...a wallpaper brush	...une brosse à maroufler

...brushes / ...des brosses

...paint trays / ...des bacs à peinture

...rollers / ...des rouleaux

where can I find... / où puis-je trouver...

...a tile cutter / ...une carrelette

...a tile cutting machine / ...un coupe-carreaux

...wall tiles / ...des carreaux pour le mur

Finding floor coverings, curtains and furniture (Track 18)

do you sell... / vendez-vous...

...carpets / ...des moquettes

...laminate flooring / ...du sol stratifié

...rugs / ...des tapis

...vinyl flooring / ...du sol vinylique

...wood flooring / ...du parquet

...blinds / ...des stores

...curtains / ...des rideaux

...curtain tracks / ...des tringles à rideaux

...net curtains / ...du voilage

we are looking for... / nous cherchons...

...an armchair / ...un fauteuil

...some chairs / ...des chaises

...a table / ...une table

...a bookcase / ...une bibliothèque

...some cupboards / ...des placards

...a sofa-bed / ...une banquette lit

...a bed / ...un lit

...a chest of drawers / ...une commode

...a wardrobe / ...une armoire

...duvets / ...des couettes

...a mattress / ...un matelas

...some pillows / ...des oreillers

Le jardin – the garden

Talking to les maçons – the builders (Track 19)

can you build…	pouvez-vous construire…
…a fence of panels	…un clôture de panneaux claustra
…a gate	…un portail
…a wall	…un mur
…a swimming pool…	…une piscine…
…with a moulded liner	…avec un bassin préformé
…with a sheet liner	…avec une bâche
the pool needs…	la piscine a besoin de…
…coping (for edge of pool)	…margelles
…a cover	…une couverture
…a pump	…une pompe
…a safety fence	…une clôture de sécurité
…a sand filter	…un filtre à sable
…some steps	…des échelles

Shopping for le jardin – the garden (Track 20)

where can I find…	où puis-je trouver…
…covers for furniture	…des housses
…deck chairs	…des transats
…flares	…des torches
…floodlights	…des projecteurs
…folding chairs	…des chaises pliantes
…garden lights	…des bornes d'allée
…a patio heater	…un parasol chauffant
…a sand pit	…un bac à sable
…a sun bed	…un bain de soleil
…a security light	…une lanterne à détecteur
…an extension lead	…une rallonge électrique
…a garden brush	…un balai cantonnier
…a hedge trimmer	…un taille-haie
…a hose	…un tuyau

...an incinerator   ...un incinérateur

...mowers   ...des tondeuses

...potting trowels   ...des déplantoirs

...a rake   ...un râteau

...a ride-on mower   ...une tondeuse autoportée

...a roller for a hosepipe ...un dévidoir

...seeds   ...des graines

...shears   ...des cisailles

...a sprinkler   ...un arroseur oscillant

...a water barrel   ...une cuve à eau

Appendix

l'investissement immobilier

Buying for investment

If you are thinking of buying property in France as an investment, think long-term, think off-plan, or think again.

At the time of writing (2010), the French economy is struggling with the aftermath of the banking crisis, the euro is shaky, and unemployment is relatively high, at around 10%, so there is little native pressure on prices. The UK property boom – which exported house price inflation to the prettier parts of much of Europe – came to a crashing halt two years back and prices in most areas are still below their peak. Having said that, in the long-term, in France as in the UK, house prices have risen ahead of inflation, and property has shown a better return than most other forms of investment – and it is reasonable to expect that to continue. Of course, you can lose money if you are not careful. There are two main dangers: paying too much in the first place, and having to sell in a hurry. I have a colleague who fell into these traps, with both feet. He bought a clifftop house in southern Brittany because he loved the view, and paid more than the house and land were worth because of it. Then three years later he needed his capital and had to sell – and couldn't find a buyer who shared his enthusiasm for the view. It was an expensive mistake. Even if you get the price right when buying, you need a sale price of 25% or so higher to show any real profit, once the fees and taxes and other costs are taken into account. On current trends, this could take a while.

Buying off-plan is offered as the way to get a short-term return on property – but it is in no way guaranteed. The theory is this: you agree to buy the apartment (which is what it normally will be) from the developer when it only exists on the plan, and you pay a 10 or 15% deposit. You will be required to come up with further payments at different stages in the building process –perhaps totalling half the purchase price. You won't need to find the rest of the cash until completion – and you may be able to sell even before that. If you get it right, the development will be so popular that people will be queuing up to buy it off you, giving you a nice quick profit. If you get it wrong, you will be left with an expensive white elephant – and since the end of the last big property boom, it's been harder to pick winners.

Holiday rentals

If you bought your French house as a holiday home, two things should follow from this: (1) it's in a nice place to have a holiday, and (2) it will be empty for much of the year. Why not rent it out to other people?

Potential rental income varies hugely, of course, depending upon the size, position and features of the house, and on the time of year, and in the quality of the marketing that brings in the visitors. A large family-sized villa with a private swimming pool in the Côte d'Azur could rent out at £2,000 or more per week in the high season; a smaller one in Brittany without a pool might fetch £400 a week. And that's not every week. So many of us now own holiday homes in France, or have friends who do, that the commercial rental market has become very competitive. Unless your property has something special, and you market it well, you should probably only expect an occupancy rate of around 15% – 8 weeks a year, and not all in the high season. That would bring in £10,000 or so for your villa on the Côte, or around £2,000 for the cottage in Britanny.

You can rent out your property through organisations like French Connections – you can also search for properties to buy in another part of this site.

You will need to find someone local to act as keyholder, cleaner, gardener, poolboy, etc., but those wages are probably about the main extra costs – your house insurance may be higher, and there will be more wear and tear on the contents.

If you want a better idea of the rental income and the occupancy rate that your house might achieve, go to the holiday rental websites, look for similar properties and check their charges and availability. (This is best done in early summer when the bookings should be largely in place.) Try these sites:

www.welcomecottages.com

www.holidaygites.co.uk

www.frenchconnections.co.uk

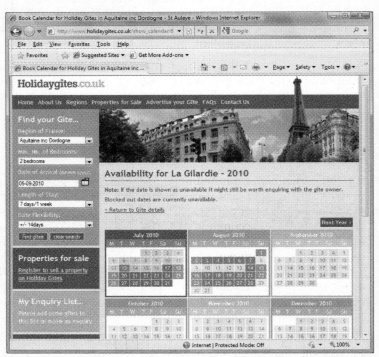

Research your market! Check the bookings of similar properties to get an idea of potential rental income. At the start of June, this 2-bedroom gitee had bookings for only five weeks in summer, and would have earned £2,500 – before costs – in total that year. Similar properties at other sites showed the same level of activity.

Gîtes as a business?

Renting to tourists can be more than just a sideline. Chateaux and bigger farmhouses with clusters of outbuildings can be converted into *gîte* complexes – subject to planning permission – and the site run as a business.

Gîtes rurals (self-catering cottages) are probably the most popular form of tourist accommodation in France, both for French residents, and for foreign tourists. Generally speaking, we Brits and other foreigners tend to expect a fairly high-standard of accommodation and equipment – and are prepared to pay for it – while the French look for something simpler, and cheaper.

If you are thinking about developing a *gîte* business, then you must look very closely at the tourist market in that area, decide on the type of accommodation you intend to provide and be very realistic in your business plan.

As a rough guide, at the time of writing (2007), a *gîte* with a pool in a popular area can bring in £120 per person per week – in the high season. Outside of that, bookings levels, and the amount that can be charged drop off rapidly.

Leaseback

If the overriding reason for buying is for investment, then you should think about a leaseback scheme. The French government introduced these about 20 years ago, as a way to encourage investment in tourist accommodation. There are several variations, but their essence is this: you buy the property, then lease it back to a management company which will maintain it and let it for you. At the end of the lease period – typically 9 years – you can either continue the arrangement, sell the property or take full possession of it. French residents are offered several tax concessions if they participate, but there are strong incentives even for non-residents:

1 You are guaranteed a minimum rental income, typically 4% to 4.5% of the non-VAT price. This is index-linked, rising in line with the official cost of construction index – currently around 2.5% p.a. – and normally reviewed every three years. The actual rents may well be much higher, depending upon

how successful the management company is in finding tenants. (As they take a percentage of the rent, they have an incentive to work hard at the lets.)

2 You can reclaim VAT from the purchase price, and VAT is currently 19.6% in France. The government position is that they will take VAT on the rent over the coming years, so can waive it on the purchase.

3 The *résidences de tourisme* are popular, with occupancy rates running at an average of 65% in recent years – significantly higher than most *gîtes* achieve.

Pierre et Vacances have been in the holiday property business since 1967 and have been the major leaseback development and management company since the scheme first started. Some of their most successful and profitable developments are in ski resorts and in cities – those in Paris normally sell out very rapidly.

4 This is 'hands-off' rental property ownership. The management company handles the cleaning, gardening, maintenance, advertising, rentals – everything. In fact, if you set up direct debits for your charges and taxes, and have rents paid directly into your bank, all you need do is read and enjoy the bank statements.

5 You own a property which will almost certainly rise in value year by year.

There are drawbacks. Leaseback was designed to be a long-term investment scheme, and may not work well over the short term as there are financial penalties on early sales.

How sure is sure?

It is important to realise that although the income is guaranteed, the guarantee is only as good as the management company. If the company folds, you could have an empty apartment that is all but unsaleable. Look for companies with good track records and solid finances.

As for any property, capital gains tax (see page 205) will be due, if you sell within the first 15 years. It could take five to ten years for the increase in value and the accumulated surplus rental income (if any) to outweigh these costs plus the costs of purchase and of servicing the mortgage. If you are confident that you will not need to sell during this timescale, then this is not a problem.

There may also be another penalty. If you sell during the first 22 years, you may have to repay a proportion of the VAT rebate – the full amount during the first two years, then reducing over the next 20. This had been a real problem until a couple of years ago, but the tax was challenged and the law clarified. You will have to repay the VAT if the buyer does not continue the leaseback. If they do continue it – and most buyers do – then the VAT allowance is carried over with the property transfer and no rebate is due.

The numbers can be very encouraging. The 4–4.5% minimum return may not be very high, but at the time of writing French banks were offering long-term mortgages with a fixed rate as low as 4%. Insurance, tax and other charges will add perhaps 1% to this, but there are two very important points to bear in mind.

The mortgage will not be on the full price of the property, and the return is index-linked. Let's see how this works out in practice.

Suppose you bought a property at £180,000, putting down a 30% (£54,000) deposit and taking out a 25-year mortgage on the rest at 4%. Your repayment would be around £8,000 p.a. – about the same as the guaranteed income – but you then need to add another £1,500 or so to cover the running costs. Assuming the current trends continue, the guaranteed income will rise by an average 2.8% each year – your running costs should also rise at about the same rate – but the mortage is fixed.

Mortgage	Costs	Income	Profit/loss	
£	£	£	£	
Year 1	£8,000	£1,500	£7,500	-£2,000
Year 10	£8,000	£1,900	£9,600	-£300
Year 20	£8,000	£2,500	£12,700	+£2,200

By year 10, the guaranteed minimum income should be about sufficient to cover both the mortgage and the costs – and the break-even point could come earlier with an effective management company and a thriving tourist industry.

Add capital gains into the equation and it looks even better. On present trends, the property should increase in value by around 7% a year. After ten years, your £180,000 property should be worth closer to £280,000 – a capital gain of £100,000, at a cost of perhaps £20,000 in accumulated costs over that time.

You can only do leaseback on properties that are built for that purpose. Most are *résidences de tourisme classée* (RTC) and almost all are in large tourist developments – either apartment blocks or chalets – in ski resorts, by the sea or in inland leisure parks, sometimes centred around golf courses. They also build them in Paris – which could be thought of as tourist development. Because they are designed for short-term occupancy, they tend to be a little smaller and to have rather less storage space than you might want in a long-term residence. Prices are typically around £150,000, but you can pay over £750,000 for luxury apartments and chalets in the top ski resorts.

Find out more

If you want to know more about leaseback, here are two sites well worth visiting:

> http://france.assetz.co.uk

Assetz, a UK company specialising in overseas property invesments, including French leasebacks

> http://www.pierreetvacances-immobilier.com

Pierre et Vacances, the leading French leaseback developer.

Taxes

Capital gains

Whatever the type of property, and whether you are resident in the house, or it is a holiday home or rental investment, if you sell it during the first 15 years of ownership you will be liable for capital gains tax. This is charged on the difference between the buying and selling prices, less the cost of any significant building work – for which you must have full receipts. If you sell within five years of purchase, you have to pay at the full rate (16%). The amount then declines steadily over the next ten years.

Here's a worked example, based on a house bought for £100,000 and which then had £50,000 spent on it in rebuilding, rewiring, plumbing and similar value-adding work. (The taxman won't allow the money spent on decorations and furnishings.)

Sold after three years for £200,000.

> Capital gain = £200,000 – £150,000 = £50,000
>
> Tax = 16% × £50,000 = £8,000

Sold after ten years for £300,000.

> Capital gain = £300,000 – £150,000 = £150,000
>
> Tax = 16% × 5/10 × £150,000 = £12,000

Income tax

If you have a rental income from your French property, then it is subject to French income tax rules. These are complex, but the crucial bit can be summarised like this:

- If your rental income is less than £5,000 then you can deduct a flat 72% and declare the rest as profit.

- If you are a non-resident, the French taxman will then take 25% of that.

So, if the income was £10,000 the taxable profit would be £2,800 (28%) and you would have to pay £700 in tax. But this is only in France. As a UK resident you may also have to pay additional tax in the UK.

Business taxes

These taxes only apply if you own the property directly, as an individual. If you own it through a company then different rules and rates apply for both capital gains and rental income. Talk to your French accountant or lawyer.

Lexicon: l'investissement – investment

achèvement (m)	completion
acompte (m)	deposit
appartement (m)	apartment
assurance (f)	insurance
bail (m)	lease
bail de gestion	management agreement
emprunt (m) logement	mortgage
gestionnaire (m)	administrator/management company
gîte (m)	home
gîte (m) rural	self-catering cottage
hypothèque (f)	mortgage
impôt (m) sur les plus-values	capital gains tax
intérêt (m)	interest
investissement (m)	investment
investissement locatif	investment for renting
loyer (m) garanti	guaranteed rent
patrimoine (m)	estate (for inheritance)

promoteur (m)   developer
résidence (f) secondaire   second home
revenue (m) foncier   rental income
TVA   VAT

English–French quick reference

apartment	appartement (m)
capital gains tax	impot (m) sur les plus-values
completion	achèvement (m)
deposit	acompte (m)
developer	promoteur (m)
estate (for inheritance)	patrimoine (m)
guaranteed rent	loyer (m) garanti
insurance	assurance (f)
interest	intérêt (m)
investment	investissement (m)
investment for renting	investissement locatif
lease	bail (m)
management agreement	bail de gestion
management company	gestionnaire (m)
mortgage	emprunt (m) logement, hypothèque (f)
rental income	revenue (m) foncier
second home	residence (f) secondaire
self-catering cottage	gîte (m) rural
VAT	TVA